**GALORE PARK**

# Junior English

# Book 3

### Andrew Hammond MA

Series Editor: Susan Elkin MA BA(Hons) Cert Ed

## www.galorepark.co.uk

Published by Galore Park Publishing Ltd
Carmelite House, 50 Victoria Embankment, London EC4Y 0D
www.galorepark.co.uk

Design and typesetting by Design Gallery
Illustrations by Gwynetth Williamson and Rosie Brooks
Printed in Italy

ISBN: 978 1 902984 80 3

First published 2006, reprinted 2007, 2008, 2009, 2010, 2011, 2012, 2013, 2014, 2016

An answer book is available to accompany this book

ISBN: 978 1 902984 85 8

Details of other Galore Park publications are available at www.galorepark.co.uk

ISEB Revision Guides, publications and examination papers may also be obtained from Galore Park.

The publishers are grateful for permission to use the extracts and photographs as follows:

Extract from Goodnight Mister Tom by Michelle Magorian (Kestrel, 1981), pages 3–4 copyright © Michelle Magorian, 1981. Reproduced by permission of
Penguin Books Ltd; extract from History of Britain: The Home Front 1939 to 1945 by Andrew Langley, published by Hamlyn Children's Books 1995, ©
1995 Reed International Books Ltd. Reproduced by permission of Egmont Books Ltd. permission sought; the poem 'Riddle' by Pamela Gillilan, The Turnspit
Dog, with illustrations by Charlotte Cory (Bloodaxe Books, 1993); extract from Biomes: Rainforest by Tony Allan. Copyright 2002 Chrysalis Children's
Books, a division of Anova Books Ltd; extract from 'Crucial New Find in Wreck of Mary Rose' by Rebecca Allison, published in The Guardian, 19 August
2003. Copyright Guardian Newspapers Limited 2003; extract from The Wreck of the Zanzibar © 1995 Michael Morpurgo. Published by Egmont Books
Limited, London and used with permission; extract from 'What is time?', source www.nmm.ac.uk © National Maritime Museum, Greenwich; extract from A
Wrinkle in Time by Madeleine L'Engle (Puffin, 1967), pages 36-37, copyright © Madeleine L'Engle, 1962. Reproduced by permission of Penguin Books Ltd;
extract from 'Keeper' by Mal Peet. Text © 2003 Mal Peet. Reproduced by permission of Walker Books Ltd, London SE11 5HJ; extract from Great Sporting
Moments by Ian Harrison is published by Cassell Illustrated priced at £16.99 and is available at all good bookstores; extract from Myths and Legends by
Brenda Ralph Lewis, and reproduced with kind permission of Brimax Publishing Ltd. All rights reserved; extract from Eyewitness Guides: Flying Machine
by Andrew Nahum (Dorling Kindersley, 2003), pages 61–62, copyright © Andrew Nahum, 2003. Reproduced by permission of Penguin Books Ltd; the
poem 'Posting Letters' by Gregory Harrison. Reproduced by kind permission of Mrs M. Harrison on behalf of the late Mr G. Harrison; extract from 'Wind
in the Willows' by Kenneth Grahame, adapted by Alan Bennett (Copyright © Forelake Ltd 1991) is reproduced by permission of PFD (www.pfd.co.uk)
on behalf of Forelake Ltd; extract from the Morgan Motor Company website (www.morgan-motor.co.uk); extract from My Family and Other Animals
by Gerald Durrell is reproduced with permission of Curtis Brown Group Limited, London on behalf of the Estate of Gerald Durrell Copyright © Gerald
Durrell 1956; extract from Journey to the River Sea by Eva Ibbotson, reproduced with permission of Macmillan, London, UK; extract from 'The Congo' by
Michael Wood, in River Journeys (ISBN 0 563 20204 1), published by the BBC Worldwide Limited. Reproduced by kind permission of Michael Wood.

Picture credits: P15 © Jack Barker / Alamy; P27 © Pepys Library, Magdalene College, Cambridge; P39 Image loaned by Salisbury Cathedral
© Photographer Steve Day; P50 Getty Images; P86 © Morgan Motor Company.

# Junior English
## Book 3

# Acknowledgements

As a Prep School Head of English I am lucky enough to be surrounded by the most discerning critics you can find: the children. My thanks to the pupils of St Andrew's School, whose enthusiastic responses (and penchant for pointing out Sir's typos) have helped me assemble this book. You're all stars.

My thanks also to Susan Elkin and Nick Oulton for their support, their advice and their continued good humour. It is refreshing to write with, and for, such kindred spirits.

Finally my thanks to my wife for her hawkish eye for detail and those mugs of tea at three in the morning.

A.H. March 2006

# Preface

This resource serves as a prequel to Susan Elkin's excellent books, *So You Really Want to Learn English Books 1, 2 and 3*.

In writing it I have kept an eye on the rigorous demands of future Common Entrance Examinations, whilst, I hope, keeping the other on the requirements of the National Curriculum and the National Literacy Strategy. As prep school teachers we are fortunate indeed: we may take the very best elements in the statutory programmes and recommended schemes that the DfES have to offer, and combine them with the preferred prep school traditions and practices.

The excerpts that are presented here may well satisfy those National Literacy Strategy text-types, and the accompanying exercises may meet (and reach beyond) the termly objectives too, but these are not their purposes. The texts you will find here, from Michelle Magorian's sublime *Goodnight Mister Tom* to Alan Bennett's marvellous adaptation of *Wind in the Willows*, have been hand-picked especially to excite, enthral, entertain and enrich the young readers in our charge. I hope you are able to derive as much pleasure in delivering this course as I found in writing it.

# Contents

## Introduction

## Chapter 1

## Chapter 2

## Chapter 3

# Chapter 4

# Chapter 5

# Chapter 6

## Chapter 7

## Chapter 8

## Chapter 9

## Chapter 10

# Introduction
## The beauty of reading

In this short collection of extracts, you will encounter a talking frog, an angel, a wartime evacuee, a time-traveller, several crocodiles and a boy who thought he could fly. Not to mention a ghost that plays football.

Such is the beauty of reading. With books you can go anywhere, be anyone and do anything. You will know (because lots of adults have told you so) that reading is important – among the most important things you will ever do, in fact. But reading is much more than a set of skills you need to practise. It is a gateway to the world. Learning to read and write can be tricky, awkward, time-consuming and perhaps even uncomfortable at times, but it is always worth it.

As you work through this book, and you read the passages and complete the exercises, you will probably have some highs and some lows. There may be some questions that make you screw your face up like a walnut, because you just can't find the answer, or others that seem so easy you want to sing. There will be some passages that you love so much you want to go out and buy the books they came from (and I strongly suggest that you do). But there may be others that you love slightly less than the teacher does (who raves on about everything anyway) and you would rather watch paint dry than read any more.

What is important is that you are reacting to what you are reading. For one of the most valuable lessons you will learn from this book, is that your opinion matters. Provided you can explain how you feel, and why you think what you do, you can't go too far wrong.

But English is unpredictable. Just when you think you've got a good foothold and you can see how far you've come and how far you've got left to climb, the ground shifts beneath your feet and you're left dangling. A spelling rule that you thought was unbreakable is broken by an exception. A phrase that you thought you understood turns out to be 'figurative' with a completely different meaning, after all. And, as I have done here, someone goes and puts an 'and' at the beginning of a sentence and you feel completely confused about what you can and can't do.

Fear not. English is tricky, yes – and there are lots of rules (and exceptions) you must learn – but above all, learning English is about learning to put your own thoughts and feelings into words – on the paper, and in conversation – in as clear and colourful a way as possible. English is personal – it's about you.

Read the passages that follow, complete the exercises, enjoy the discussions and role-plays and write some wonderful stories. But more than that, use this short book as a way of reminding yourself that you can 'do English' (because you've been 'doing it' ever since you were born). From the moment you were able to make yourself understood, you've been using words to make sense of the wonderful, amazing, mesmerising, startling and miraculous world around you!

So just keep doing it.

# Chapter 1

## A long way from home

When young William Beech and his fellow evacuees turn up in the village of Little Weirwold, elderly resident Tom Oakley is less than overjoyed to see them.

'Yes,' said Tom bluntly, on opening the front door. 'What do you want?'

A harassed middle-aged woman in a green coat and felt hat stood on his step. He glanced at the armband on her sleeve. She gave him an awkward smile.

5　'I'm the Billeting Officer for this area,' she began.

'Oh yes, and what's that got to do wi'me?'

She flushed slightly. 'Well, Mr, Mr...'

'Oakley. Thomas Oakley.'

'Ah, thank you, Mr Oakley.' She paused and took a deep breath.

10　'Mr Oakley, with the declaration of war imminent...'

Tom waved his hand. 'I knows all that. Get to the point. What d'you want?' He noticed a small boy at her side.

'It's him I've come about,' she said. 'I'm on my way to your village hall with the others.'

15　'What others?'

She stepped to one side. Behind the large iron gate which stood at the end of the graveyard were a small group of children. Many of them were filthy and very poorly clad. Only a handful had a blazer or coat.

They all looked bewildered and exhausted. One tiny dark-haired girl in
20　the front was hanging firmly on to a new teddybear. The woman touched the boy at her side and pushed him forward.

'There's no need to tell me,' said Tom. 'It's obligatory and it's for the war effort.'

'You are entitled to choose your child, I know,' began the woman apologetically.

25 Tom gave a snort.

'But,' she continued, 'his mother wants him to be with someone who's religious or near a church. She was quite adamant. Said she would only let him be evacuated if he was.'

'Was what?' asked Tom impatiently.

30 'Near a church.'

Tom took a second look at the child. The boy was thin and sickly-looking, pale with limp, sandy hair and dull grey eyes.

'His name's Willie,' said the woman.

Willie, who had been staring at the ground, looked up. Round his neck,
35 hanging from a piece of string, was a cardboard label. It read 'William Beech'.

Tom was well into his sixties, a healthy, robust, stockily-built man with a head of thick white hair. Although he was of average height, in Willie's eyes he was a towering giant with skin like coarse, wrinkled brown paper and a voice like thunder.

40 He glared at Willie. 'You'd best come in,' he said abruptly.

The woman gave a relieved smile. 'Thank you so much,' she said, and she backed
45 quickly away and hurried down the tiny path towards the other children. Willie watched
50 her go.

'Come on in,' repeated Tom harshly. 'I ent got all day.'

*(From Goodnight Mister Tom by Michelle Magorian)*

# Exercise 1.1 ✏

Answer the following questions using full sentences.

1. Why has the Billeting Officer called at Tom Oakley's door?

2. What does the word *harassed* mean in line 2?

3. Do you think Tom is pleased to see his visitors? Write down two words from the passage that tell you how he feels about being disturbed.

4. What was the special request Willie's mother made concerning her son's evacuation?

5. Describe Willie's first impressions of Tom Oakley as they meet on the doorstep.

6. Write a sentence to describe Tom's character, based on what you have read. You will need to think carefully about what he says and how he says it.

. . . . . . . . . . . . . . . . . . . . . . . . . . . . . . . . . . . . . . . . . . . . . . . . . . . . . .

## Difficult times

'They labelled me, addressed me and packed me off to the country.' This is one man's memory of being evacuated at the start of the war. He was only nine years old at the time. Like thousands of other children, he spent most of the war living far away from his parents.

5 Wartime was very frightening and confusing for young children. Many of those in towns were evacuated to areas away from the dangers of German bombers. They were taken away by train, bus or even boat. They stayed in private houses in villages or country towns.

Many children never left the cities. They were soon joined by young
10 evacuees who had grown homesick and went back to their parents. But life in the heavily bombed cities, such as London, Manchester, Liverpool and Plymouth, could be much more terrifying. Families spent the nights in public air-raid shelters, or in tiny 'Anderson' shelters in their gardens.

Sweets were rationed, and there were fewer toys in the shops. But
15 town children soon got used to playing among the ruined buildings and streets blocked with rubble. They competed with each other in making collections of 'trophies' – pieces from bombs or crashed aircraft. Other

collections helped in the war effort. Some children gathered scrap metal, such as old pots and pans. This was taken to dumps. It was melted down 20 and could be used in the manufacture of aircraft and weapons.

*(From The Homefront by Andrew Langley)*

# Exercise 1.2

Answer the following questions as fully as you can.

1. Why were children evacuated from cities to the countryside?

2. Name the three methods of transport used to move the children out of the cities to safety.

3. Why did some evacuees return home to their parents?

4. What were 'trophies' (line 17)?

5. What happened to the scrap metal that the children found amongst the rubble?

6. Write short definitions for the following words: (a) *evacuee* (line 10); (b) *homesick* (line 10); (c) *rationed* (line 14).

# Exercise 1.3

Your turn to write:

1. Imagine you are William Beech. Write a short extract from an imaginary diary, in which you describe the day you arrived in Little Weirwold and met Tom Oakley.

2. What do you think Tom and Willie say to one another when they enter Tom's house? Extend the passage to include a conversation that might take place between Tom and his new house guest after the Billeting Officer has left them.

3. Design the front page of a newspaper dated 10th September 1939, in which news of the first evacuations is reported. Choose one major city (London, Birmingham or Plymouth, for example) and describe the scenes

as the children say goodbye to their mothers and board the trains that will take them away to the countryside.

4. Imagine you are one of the city children who stayed at home with your parents during the second world war. Write a few paragraphs to describe the fun, and the hardship, as you amuse yourself by hunting for trophies amongst the rubble.

5. Would you like to have been an evacuee? Would you have missed home? Write a paragraph or two in which you describe your own thoughts and feelings about being evacuated.

## Learning about language
### Capital letters and full stops

Every sentence begins with a capital letter and ends in either a full stop (.), a question mark (?) or an exclamation mark (!).

*I am going to the beach today.*

*Would you like to come too?*

*You bet I would!*

The first example is an ordinary sentence – or statement – in which the speaker announces he or she is going to the beach. In the second, the speaker asks a question, so the sentence needs a question mark. In the third example, the sentence is an exclamation, said boldly and with plenty of enthusiasm, so it needs an exclamation mark.

## Exercise 1.4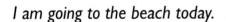

Write out the following sentences adding capital letters where you think they are needed. Then decide whether each one requires a full stop, question mark or exclamation mark.

1. the Billeting Officer arrived at Tom's door

2. can you look after an evacuee

3. I've told you I can't

4. the children looked tired and hungry

5. what a sorry sight

6. have you travelled far

By looking for full stops and capital letters, we can see where one sentence finishes and another one begins. Without these tools, our writing would be very confusing to read. Carving up paragraphs into different sentences allows the reader to receive information in small units, without becoming too confused.

# Exercise 1.5

Copy this paragraph in which William Beech is taken into Tom Oakley's care. You will need to add all the necessary full stops and capital letters.

nervously, Willie followed Tom into a dark hallway it took a few seconds for his eyes to adjust from the brilliant sunshine he had left to the comparative darkness of the cottage he could just make out the shapes of a few coats hanging on some wooden pegs and two pairs of boots standing below.

## Building sentences

A sentence is a complete statement that makes sense on its own. It begins with a capital letter and ends with either a full stop (.), question mark (?) or exclamation mark (!).

Here are some other rules for sentence-building:

- Every sentence must contain at least one *verb*. For example:

  He *glanced* at the armband on her sleeve.
      *verb*

- A sentence contains a *subject* and usually (but not always) an *object*. The *subject* is the noun or pronoun that the sentence is about. The *subject* performs the action in a sentence. The *object* is the noun or pronoun to whom, or to which, the action is being done.

For example:

Tom waved his *hand*.
subject          object

*She* flushed slightly.
subject     *(no object)*

- The *verb* and the *object* in a sentence are sometimes known as the *predicate*. Every sentence must have a *subject* and a *predicate*.

For example:

| Tom | waved his hand |
|---|---|
| *subject* | *predicate* |

# Exercise 1.6

Copy the following sentences – taken from the passages above – and underline the *verb(s)* in each one. There may be more than one, so look carefully.

1. She gave him an awkward smile.

2. She paused and took a deep breath.

3. The woman touched the boy at her side and pushed him forward.

4. Some children gathered scrap metal, such as old pots and pans.

5. Sweets were rationed, and there were fewer toys in the shops.

# Exercise 1.7

Copy the following sentences and underline the *subject* in each one.

1. They all looked bewildered and exhausted.

2. Tom gave a snort.

3. Wartime was very frightening and confusing.

4. Many children never left the cities.

5. But town children soon got used to playing among the ruined buildings and streets blocked with rubble.

# Exercise 1.8 ✏️

Some of the following sentences contain an *object* and some don't. Copy each sentence and either underline the *object*, or write *'(no object)'* at the end of it.

1. He noticed a small boy at her side.

2. She flushed slightly.

3. One tiny dark-haired girl in the front was cuddling a new teddybear.

4. He glared at Willie.

5. The boy was thin and sickly-looking.

· · · · · · · · · · · · · · · · · · · · · · · · · · · · · · · · · · · · · · · ·

# Can you spell?

## Homophones

Some words may sound alike but have different meanings or spellings. Take 'see' and 'sea' for example, or 'time' and 'thyme'.

We call these words *homophones*. Other examples include:

*plane / plain*

*key / quay*

*blew / blue*

If we are not careful, sometimes we may put the wrong word in a sentence, even though it sounds correct. For example, *there* and *their* often cause confusion. (Even *they're*, the contracted form of 'they are', can turn up in the wrong place.)

Be sure you know the differences in the *meanings* and *spellings* of homophones.

# Exercise 1.9

Write two separate sentences for each of the following pairs of homophones to show that you understand the different meanings:

1. night / knight

2. weight / wait

3. flower / flour

4. deer / dear

5. medal / meddle

# Exercise 1.10

Copy the following sentences, replacing the homophone with a different one if you think it is wrong. Beware: not all the homophones are incorrect.

1. We were asked if we *wood* like to accompany them on holiday.

2. Rosie explained that *there* were no seats left in the theatre.

3. Father did not wish to make a *seen*, so he said the soup was fine.

4. Grandad moved to the countryside for some *piece* and quiet.

5. Jacob's feet had *grown* considerably and his old shoes felt uncomfortable.

# Exercise 1.11

Now it's your turn to think of some homophones. Try to think of *five* more pairs of homophones and write sentences to show that you understand the different meanings. Be sure to spell each homophone correctly.

# Speaking and listening

1. Work with a partner. Imagine you are two evacuees, sitting on a train, leaving your homes in the city behind you. Where are you going? What will the countryside be like? Will you make any new friends? Share your thoughts and feelings in character. Then perform your conversations to the class.

2. Work in a group of about four. Two of you imagine you are pupils in a small village school. The year is 1940 and you have just welcomed two evacuees from the city into your school (played by the other members in your group). Rehearse and perform a short scene in which you try to make the evacuees feel welcome.

3. Find out more about evacuation during the war and prepare a short talk, or presentation, for your class. You can find lots of interesting information on the Internet, or from books, magazines and CD ROMs. Prepare some short notes or bullet points to help you present your talk.

4. Work with a partner. Share your views about staying away from home. Have you ever stayed away for a few days? Did you feel homesick? Were you able to keep busy so that you didn't miss home too much?

5. In larger groups, or as a class, join in a 'hot-seating' session, in which volunteers take turns to sit in a chair at the front (known as the 'hot seat') and answer questions in the character of an evacuee just like William Beech.

# Have you read?

The following stories involve tales of evacuation, war and courage.

*The Silver Sword* by Ian Serraillier (Red Fox)
*Hitler's Canary* by Sandi Toksvig (Doubleday)
*When Hitler Stole Pink Rabbit* by Judith Kerr (Collins)
*Tamar* by Mal Peet (Walker Books)
*The Machine Gunners* by Robert Westall (Macmillan Children's Books)
*Carrie's War* by Nina Bawden (Puffin Modern Classics)
*War Boy* by Michael Foreman (Puffin Books)

*Evacuation (At Home in World War II)* by Stewart Ross (Evans Brothers)
*Chain of Fire* by Beverley Naidoo (Puffin Books)
*I Am David* by Anne Holm (Mammoth)
*The Amazing Story of Adolphus Tips* by Michael Morpurgo (Harper Collins)

# Other things to do...

- Write a poem entitled 'Leaving Home', in which you describe the railway journey for an evacuee as he or she leaves the city, bound for a strange new place in the countryside. Think about what the evacuee sees, hears and feels as the train whisks him or her away.

- During the war many foods and other supplies had to be 'rationed' to make sure that there was enough to go around. Find out more about rationing, using the Internet, CD ROMs and books. Use key questions to guide your research, such as: Which foods were rationed? What did ration books look like? How many ration coupons was each family entitled to?

- Find out more about Michelle Magorian's classic story, *Goodnight Mister Tom*. There is an excellent film of the story and an audio cassette version too.

# Chapter 2

## Think of a world

You could slake a small thirst
from my cup or take
my smooth worry bead
of a seed and cast up
5  slow centuries of growth. I'm planned
to outlast you, stand high
above you. Make me, raw stuff
for your saws, into stairs,
beams, doors, shelves, rough
10  firewood, fine chairs. I am air
for your breath, I am loam
for growth. You, who need Earth
for your home, must revere, must spare
me; there will be no birth,
15  only a dwindling to death without
me and my kind. We are beacons;
we flare to guide, to warn.
Watch our green burning; while we
live you come to no harm.

*(Riddle, by Pamela Gillilan, Turnspit Dog)*

# Exercise 2.1 🖉

Read the poem by Pamela Gillilan and then answer the following questions using complete sentences.

1. Who, or what, is speaking in the poem? (In other words, from whose viewpoint is it written?)

2. Name three ways in which we humans rely on the speaker.

3. What do you think is meant by the phrase, 'we flare to guide'?

4. In what ways might the speaker be threatened by Man?

**5.** Find dictionary definitions for the following words: (a) *slake* (line 1); (b) *loam* (line 11); (c) *revere* (line 13); (d) *beacon* (line 16).

**6.** Look again at the words 'watch our green burning' in line 18. Do you think this is an important line? When we use wood for firewood isn't it usually brown or yellow in colour, never green? Could the poet be referring to living trees? Write a sentence or two to describe your reaction to this line.

· · · · · · · · · · · · · · · · · · · · · · · · · · · · · · · · · · · · · · · · · · · · · · · ·

## Zeca's world

Zeca is 15 years old and lives in the Amazon rainforest. She belongs to the Yanomami people, who occupy a vast belt of almost uninterrupted woodland near the Brazil-Venezuela border. Her days are spent in and around the yano, the ring-shaped communal house which she and her parents share with a dozen other families.

'The rainforest is our home, the only one we know. It gives us all we need — food to eat, medicines when we are sick, wood and palm fronds to build the yano. We grow cotton to make the aprons and waistbands that we wear, and there's a forest plant called urucu that provides the red dye we paint on our
5    faces and bodies to make ourselves look beautiful. We use brightly-coloured

flowers and feathers to adorn our heads and arms, and shells from the riverside to make necklaces.

Days are mostly like one another, except for the special times when we go to a neighbouring yano for a feast. I wake with the sun, but there's no
10  rush to get up; maybe I'll eat some papaya fruit, and then get back into the hammock until the family are up and about. Most days I go to the gardens with my mother to help with the weeding, and we make trips out into the forest where she shows me which wild fruit and berries are good to eat. She has taught me everything I know: how to thread necklaces, where
15  to find crabs and crayfish by the riverside, how to make bread from the vegetable called manioc.

Yet my mother seems worried. The other adults talk of the foreigners who have come with huge machines to cut down trees not far from our village. They brought diseases with them, which killed some Yanomami in a nearby
20  yano. We hope they don't come here. They would spoil everything.'

*(From Rainforest by Tony Allan)*

. . . . . . . . . . . . . . . . . . . . . . . . . . . . . . . . . . . . . . . . . . . . . . . . . .

# Exercise 2.2 ✏️

Read the extract from *Rainforest* and then answer the following questions using complete sentences.

1. Where do the Yanomami people live?

2. What is a *yano*?

3. What two things does the rainforest provide for the Yanomami people to help them survive?

4. Why is the urucu plant important to Zeca's tribe?

5. (a) Zeca does not attend school, so how does she learn?

   (b) What sorts of skills has she learnt?

6. Explain as fully as you can – and in your own words – why Zeca's mother seems worried.

7.  Use a dictionary to find the correct meanings of the following words:
    (a) *dye* (line 4); (b) *adorn* (line 6); (c) *hammock* (line 11); (d) *foreigners*
    (line 17).

# Exercise 2.3

Your turn to write:

1.  Imagine you are trekking through the rainforest when you stumble across
    some Yanomami people, living in a giant yano. Write part of an imaginary
    travel journal in which you describe your first impressions of this
    fascinating rainforest tribe.

2.  Have you ever lain beneath the branches of a tree and looked up?  You'll
    find a truly amazing and intricate pattern of leaves. Write a poem in which
    you celebrate the beauty of trees and their important role in our world.

3.  Write a story in which a group of friends go trekking together in the
    rainforest.  Soon they become lost and fear that they may never find their
    way out of the dense jungle. Then help comes from a Yanomami hunter
    who stumbles across them. What will happen next?

4.  Write part of an imaginary diary describing a day in the life of Zeca and
    her family.  Pretend that you are Zeca or her brother.  Describe the place
    where you live and the skills you learn each day in the forest. You may
    wish to do some extra research first, by looking up the Yanomami people
    on Internet websites and in geography books.

# Learning about language

## Noun revision

A noun is a naming word – it tells us the name of
a thing. There are several types of noun:

common noun      a **table**, a **shoe**

proper noun      **Mrs Bakewell, Norwich**

collective noun      a **pack** of wolves, a **herd** of cows

abstract noun     **courage, morning**

compound noun    a **notebook**, a **holidaymaker**

## Compound nouns

I'm sure you know about most of these types of noun, but let us just look for a moment at the last type, the compound noun. Sometimes we combine two separate words together to make one whole word – called a **compound** word. Your **bedroom**, for example, is the room in which you have your bed.

Or, if a hairdresser cuts your hair for you, you have had a **haircut**.

bed + room = bedroom

hair + cut = haircut

Compound nouns are surprisingly common. If a noun can be divided into two recognisable smaller words, it is probably a compound noun.

. . . . . . . . . . . . . . . . . . . . . . . . . . . . . . . . . . . . . . . . . . . . . . . .

# Exercise 2.4 ✏

The following sentences contain examples of different sorts of noun. Copy each one and then identify the type of noun that appears in bold print. The first has been done for you.

1. Evelyn lives in a large **forest**. (common noun)

2. A **flock** of birds flew over the forest clearing.

3. Zeca belongs to the **Yanomami** tribe.

4. Zeca and her family grow cotton to make aprons and **waistbands**.

5. Most days are spent in the **garden**, helping with the weeding.

6. The **peace** of the rainforest may be spoiled by foreigners who come to cut down trees.

# Exercise 2.5 ✏

In the following sentences the names of the people and places – known as proper nouns – have lost their capital letters, so that they look like ordinary common nouns. Write out each sentence, giving the proper nouns the capital letters they need.

1. The yanomami people live in the rainforests of brazil.

2. The amazon rainforest of south america is the largest forest in the world.

3. It takes a long time to travel from great britain to south america.

4. Sometimes zeca helps her mother with the weeding.

5. The country of brazil shares a border with venezuela.

· · · · · · · · · · · · · · · · · · · · · · · · · · · · · · · · · · · · · · · · · · ·

# Exercise 2.6 ✏

Write out the following sentences and underline the compound noun in each.

1. Zeca made aprons and waistbands for the other villagers.

2. Tom packed his suitcase and set off for South America.

3. Deep in the rainforest, the Yanomami people built their new yano.

4. Zeca found some beautiful shells along the riverside.

5. Tom peered out of the aeroplane window to see vast stretches of woodland below.

· · · · · · · · · · · · · · · · · · · · · · · · · · · · · · · · · · · · · · · · · · ·

# Exercise 2.7 ✏

Now see if you can complete the following compound nouns, using the clues that appear next to them.

1. motor....        (faster than a bicycle)

2. after....        (from midday to evening)

3. clock....        (driven by springs and cogs)

4. hedge.... (too prickly to touch)

5. light.... (to keep ships safe at night)

6. bag.... (played by a man in a skirt)

7. chatter.... (too much talking)

8. black.... (handy with a hammer)

9. sweet.... (valentine)

10. grape.... (too sour for me)

## Adjectives

Sometimes known as describing words, **adjectives** usually describe nouns.

For example:

a **beautiful** sunset

the **friendly** policeman

an **ancient** ruin

Adjectives provide interest and information. Without them our sentences would be very dull and lifeless.

. . . . . . . . . . . . . . . . . . . . . . . . . . . . . . . . . . . . . . . . . . . . . . .

## Exercise 2.8

Can you think of an adjective for each of the following letters?  Write them in a list.

a _____        p _____

d _____        s _____

g _____        t _____

i _____        v _____

m _____        y _____

# Exercise 2.9 ✏

Now see if you can think of some interesting adjectives to accompany the following nouns.

1. some _____ jewellery

2. a _____ banquet

3. the _____ church

4. two _____ apples

5. a _____ storm

When selecting adjectives to accompany nouns in a sentence it is a good idea to avoid the more ordinary words that are overused, like 'nice' and 'big'. A **thesaurus** can be a very useful tool for finding more interesting adjectives with similar meanings (these are called synonyms and we shall explore them in a later chapter).

. . . . . . . . . . . . . . . . . . . . . . . . . . . . . . . . . . . . . . . . . . . . .

# Exercise 2.10 ✏

Copy the following sentences and replace the adjectives in bold with a more interesting alternative. You may use a thesaurus if you have one handy.

1. The **tall** trees towered over the people like **friendly** giants.

2. The Yanomami tribe built a **big** yano in a **quiet** part of the forest.

3. Living in the forest was **fun**, but there was lots of **hard** work to do.

4. The **hot** sun beat down on the **tired** villagers.

# Can you spell?

## Adding adjective endings to nouns

Some adjectives are made by adding extra letters to the end of nouns so that the word changes its function. The extra letters we add are called a 'suffix' and the original word is called the 'root word'. Here are some common examples:

| noun (root word) | adjective (with suffix added) |
|---|---|
| help | help**ful** |
| peace | peace**ful** |
| topic | topic**al** |
| music | music**al** |
| cloud | cloud**y** |
| dust | dust**y** |
| sun | sun**ny** |
| fog | fo**ggy** |

Notice how, in the final two examples, the last letter of the noun is doubled before adding a 'y' to the end.

. . . . . . . . . . . . . . . . . . . . . . . . . . . . . . . . . . . . . . . . . . . . . . . . . . . .

# Exercise 2.11

Copy the following nouns and then add a suffix to each to turn it into an adjective. Be careful: some of the nouns will need double letters, others won't.

1. fun
2. colour
3. mist
4. logic
5. hope
6. rest
7. joy
8. love
9. cynic
10. dirt

Sometimes you need to remove a letter or two from a root word before you can change it into an adjective:

grim**e** – grim**y**     nois**e** – nois**y**     ang**er** – ang**ry**

# Exercise 2.12 ✏

Now see if you can identify the root word (or noun) in the following adjectives. Copy each one and then write the original noun next to it. The first one has been done for you.

1. hazy (haze)
2. rainy
3. comical
4. revengeful
5. cheesy

6. beastly
7. delightful
8. gusty
9. idiotic
10. interesting

# Speaking and listening

1. Hot-seating: Take turns to sit in the 'hot seat' – a chair at the front of the class – and answer questions from your friends in the role of Zeca or another member of the Yanomami tribe of Brazil.

2. Group role-play: Arrange yourselves into groups of about four or six. One half of your group can pretend to be Yanomami people, living a peaceful life in the rainforest; the others can be foreigners, coming in to cut down the trees. What will happen when you meet? Will you be able to resolve your differences?

3. Hold a class debate in which you write speeches that support or oppose the following motion: *This house believes that all people of the rainforest should be left to live in peace.* Your first reaction to this may be to say 'of course they should', but think about ways in which the outside world could help them – with modern medicines to help them fight diseases and modern equipment to assist them in their work.

4. Find out about other tribes who live in rainforests around the world. You could begin with the Iban people of Borneo. Work with a partner and put together a short presentation to share the information you have found. You may choose to use posters and pictures to make your talk more interesting and colourful.

# Have you read?

The following list includes stories and non-fiction books about the rainforest.

*Mrs Parrot's Rainforest Lessons* by Michael Cox (Scholastic)
*Rainforest* by Helen Sharman (Dorling Kindersley)
*The Vanishing Rainforest* by Richard Platt (et al.) (Frances Lincoln Publishers)
*Rainforest People* by Edward Parker (Hodder Wayland)
*Spirit in the Rainforest* by Eric Wilson (Orca Book Publishers)
*Journey into the Rainforest* by Tim Knight (Oxford University Press)
*The Most Beautiful Roof in the World* by K. Lasky and C. Knight, (Gulliver Green)
*Rainforest Explorer* by Sue Nicholson (Marshall Editions)
*Tail of a Rainforest: Kiko and the Jungle Jewels* by Megan Koss (Author House)
*Rainforest Animals* by Paul Hess (Zero to Ten)

. . . . . . . . . . . . . . . . . . . . . . . . . . . . . . . . . . . . . . . . . . . .

# Other things to do...

- Research the subject of trees – particularly how they keep us, and our planet, alive. How do they create the climate that sustains us? What would the earth be like without trees? Would we be able to live on it? Think particularly about the air we breathe.

- Find out more about how the Yanomami people – and other tribes like them – are being threatened by deforestation (cutting down vast areas of rainforest). There are lots of websites, books and encyclopaedias that can offer you information. Once you have found some interesting facts, put together a poster, telling people what is happening to the rainforest and explaining how they can help.

# Chapter 3

## The wreck

It is 1907 and life on the Scilly Isles is bleak and difficult for Laura and her family. When a ship is unexpectedly wrecked against the rocks at Tearing Ledges, the islanders race to see if they can offer help in return for any valuables they can find.

### December 9th

I don't know where to begin. Granny May is still asleep. She wakes from time to time and looks up at me fondly. I've told her again and again what's happened today. She just smiles and pats my hand. I hope she
5   understands, but I'm not sure she does. I'm not sure I do.

Mother sent me out early as usual to fetch back some limpets or whatever I could find. It was too rough again to fish from the rocks. The storm was worse than ever. There must have been a dozen of us out doing the same thing on Great Porth, when someone saw the sail. The rain was coming
10  in hail squalls[1], driving into my face so hard that I could scarcely open my eyes. One sail became four, white against the black storm clouds. The ship was beating her way past Seal Rock towards the Tearing Ledges, making no headway in the teeth of a gale. We all knew what was going to happen. We'd seen it before. A ship about to founder staggers before she falls. A
15  huge wave broke over her stern and she did not come upright again. She lay on her side and wallowed in the waves.

The cry went up from all around. 'Wreck! Wreck!'

I raced home and met Father and the Chief coming up the
20  track at a run.

'Is it true?' cried Father, anxiously. 'Have we got a wreck?'

When we reached the
25  boathouse they were already hauling the gig[2] down into the surf. Time and again, the crew

leapt in and we pushed them out, up to our waists in the icy sea, and time
and again they were driven back by the waves. In the end she was caught
30  broadside on, capsized and everyone was upturned into the sea. After that
everyone wanted to give up, everyone except the Chief.

'Rushy Bay!' he shouted, confidently. 'Nothing else for it. We'll be out of
the wind. We'll launch her there!'

But no one would hear of it until the schoolteacher came running along
35  the beach towards us, breathless.

'There's men in the sea,' she said, 'we saw them from Samson Hill. The
ship's gone on the rocks.'

*(Adapted from The Wreck of the Zanzibar by Michael Morpurgo, 1995)*

[1]**squalls** = *gusts of wind and rain*          [2]**gig** = *a lightweight rowing boat*

# Exercise 3.1

Answer these questions using full sentences.

1.  How does Granny react to Laura's news of the day's events?

2.  Why did Mother send Laura out?

3.  Why was she unable to fish from the rocks on that day?

4.  Describe the effect that the 'huge wave' (lines 15) has on the ship.

5.  What caused everyone to want to give up?

6.  Replace the words underlined with an alternative word or phrase that
    has the same meaning. You may use a thesaurus to help you.
    (a) driving into my face (line 10); (b) hauling the gig (line 26); (c) the icy
    sea (line 28).

## A historic find

When the remains of King Henry's flagship, Mary Rose, were first discovered on the bottom of the sea bed, no one could have imagined just how much treasure was there. Then, the world watched as the wreck was gently raised to the surface. Now, twenty years later, divers are still hopeful that the last remaining pieces of the ship will be found.

Dive 29 began like all the rest. A slow descent followed by an even slower passage through the murky haze, 10 metres below the surface, as the buddy team groped along the sea bed in search of evidence of a disaster nearly 500 years old.

5  As they sifted blindly through the mounds of silt for the ninth day in a row, a chance brush against a piece of timber brought the routine to an abrupt end and yielded a prize more valuable than anyone had hoped for.

Two decades after three-quarters of the Tudor warship *Mary Rose* was dramatically raised from the Solent, marine archaeologists revisiting the
10  site believe they may have discovered its missing front section.

Experts who have been diving the wreck off Portsmouth for the last month believe the five-metre-long piece of wood they discovered by chance, on July 31st, could be the missing front stem of the ship's keel.

15 They believe this stem could be attached to the bowcastle, the fortified front of Henry VIII's flagship, which has been shown in reconstruction drawings as a fanciful turreted structure like a miniature medieval castle.

If this is true, it means that the final jigsaw piece of *Mary Rose* has been found and a complete cross section of the ship, which sank on her way into battle in 1545 within sight of the King standing on the shore, has now
20 been discovered.

Alex Hildred, the dive's project manager, said that if the find was confirmed it would be 'the most important maritime archaeological find in England in the last 20 years.'

She added: 'It gives us a chance to put the front of the *Mary Rose* on. It is
25 hugely exciting and vitally important.'

The chief executive of the Mary Rose Trust, John Lippiett, said the find had gone beyond all expectations. 'It is an extraordinary discovery. Are we going to find an awful lot more under the silt? The chances are yes because I am an optimist. What we have found is in remarkable condition,'
30 he added.

'We do not know the real construction of the bowcastle. There have been reconstruction drawings which contain a lot of licence. If it is there, it is the only example in the world. This revolutionary design was the forerunner to modern-day warships. It is of enormous significance in
35 maritime archaeology and naval history.'

The Prince of Wales, who dived the wreck site in the 1970s and is president of the trust, said he was thrilled by the latest find. 'The story of the *Mary Rose* has intrigued generations of people, and I am confident this latest discovery will reignite people's interest in the gem of Tudor maritime
40 history,' he said.

*(By Rebecca Allison, published in The Guardian on Tuesday 19ᵗʰ August 2003)*

# Exercise 3.2 ✏

Answer the following questions using full sentences.

1. Explain what the 'historic find' actually is.

2. Using your own words as far as possible, describe the conditions the divers had to endure ten metres below the surface.

3. Why do you think the team is particularly excited about this find? What does it mean for the *Mary Rose*?

4. Why do you think a quotation from Prince Charles has been included?

5. Use a dictionary to find definitions for the following words: (a) *yielded* (line 7); (b) *fortified* (line 14); (c) *optimist* (line 29); (d) *forerunner* (line 34).

# Exercise 3.3 ✏

Your turn to write:

1. Re-read the extract from *The Wreck of the Zanzibar* and then plan, and write, a poem in which you describe the sight of the ship breaking up in the storm, the waves lashing against the side, and its white sails standing out against the blackened skies. Try to use lots of interesting adjectives and verbs.

2. Write your own story about a ship which breaks up in a storm, leaving a few survivors to fend for themselves on a desert island. What will happen to them? Will a ship see them and send a rescue team, or will they spend the rest of their days on tropical shores?

3. Look again at the passage entitled *A Historic Find*. Imagine you are one of the crew members on Dive 29. Write an entry in your diary about how you felt when you first realised you may have discovered the missing piece of the *Mary Rose* jigsaw. Begin by describing the descent to the bottom and the difficult conditions you had to work in.

4. Compose a piece of factual writing that could accompany the bowcastle in the Mary Rose Museum. You will need to explain to visitors how and when the missing piece was first discovered and why it was such an important breakthrough for researchers or maritime archaeologists.

**5.** Write a story of your own entitled *The Find of a Lifetime* in which an important discovery is made somewhere around the world. It may be under the sea, high up in the mountains or buried deep below the earth. The discovery will come at the end of a long and gruelling expedition and, whatever it may be, it will attract attention around the world.

# Learning about language

## Speech marks

As their name suggests, **speech marks** are used to mark the words that are spoken by someone in a piece of writing like a story or a diary. They are sometimes called quotation marks or inverted commas.

Speech marks surround the actual words spoken by a character. When writing by hand we usually use a pair of speech marks each time: " "

But when authors write stories in print, they often use single speech marks: ' '

The first word that is spoken by a person always has a capital letter, even if it comes midway through a sentence:

She added, 'It gives us a chance to put the front of the Mary Rose on.'

If the words spoken are broken by more of the story, you do not use a capital letter when continuing them:

'The Mary Rose,' she said, 'is one of our greatest treasures.'

Before a speech closes, there must always be a mark of punctuation – a full stop, question mark, exclamation mark or comma.

Always begin a new paragraph when there is a change of speaker. Then the reader can follow when someone different is speaking in a conversation (sometimes called 'dialogue').

# Exercise 3.4 ✏

Copy each of the following sentences and add the missing punctuation. Include speech marks, full stops, question marks, exclamation marks or commas.

1. There's men in the sea she said I saw them from Samson Hill

2. Is it true cried Father Have we got a wreck

3. Rushy Bay he shouted, confidently

4. Chief executive of the Mary Rose Trust, John Lippiett, said it is an extraordinary discovery

5. The story of the *Mary Rose* has intrigued generations of people said the Prince

## Adverbs in speech

Look at the following sentence, taken from the first passage.

*'Rushy Bay!' he shouted,* **confidently**. *'Nothing else for it. We'll be out of the wind. We'll launch her there!'*

Here we learn not only what the Chief says but also *how* he says it. The adverb *confidently* tells us more about the character of the Chief. When everyone else wanted to give up, he remained confident.

An adverb adds to the meaning of the verb, which in the example above is the word *shouted*. Using adverbs in speech to accompany words like *said* and *replied* helps to build a more interesting picture for the reader and brings the speakers to life.

Many adverbs end in 'ly', like *angrily*, *quietly* and *happily*.

# Exercise 3.5 ✏

Copy the following sentences and underline the adverbs in each one.

1. 'Is it true?' cried Father, anxiously. 'Have we got a wreck?'

2. 'Hello, dear,' Granny May said sweetly.

3. 'Will you go and collect some limpets?' asked Mother, politely.

4. 'This could be the most important maritime archaeological find in England in the last 20 years,' he said proudly.

5. 'It's hugely exciting and vitally important,' she added enthusiastically.

## Exercise 3.6

Now see if you can use each of the following adverbs in a line of speech of your own. Remember to use speech marks correctly too.

loudly        joyously        quickly        mischievously        slowly

# Can you spell?

## Adding adverb endings to adjectives

Many, though not all, adverbs are formed by adding '-ly' to the end of an adjective. For example:

slow – slow**ly**;  quick – quick**ly**;  eloquent – eloquent**ly**;  gallant – gallant**ly**

There are other adjectives, however, that require some extra changes before they can be made into adverbs.

Try to learn the following rules:

- If an adjective ends in '-y', change the 'y' to an 'i' and then add '-ly' as normal. e.g. happy – happ**i**ly; pretty – prett**i**ly; noisy – nois**i**ly; angry – angr**i**ly

- Usually, if an adjective ends in '-ic', we add '-ally' to the end.
  e.g. sarcastic – sarcastic**ally**; fantastic – fantastic**ally**; ironic – ironic**ally** (But there are exceptions, like: public – publicly.)

- If an adjective already ends in '-l', still add '-ly' as usual.

  Note it gives you a double 'l'. e.g.
  beautiful – beautiful**ly**;
  usual – usual**ly**;
  respectful – respectful**ly**

# Exercise 3.7 ✏

Copy these adjectives and next to each one write the adverb that is formed from it.

1. merry
2. peaceful
3. warm
4. pathetic
5. pleasing

· · · · · · · · · · · · · · · · · · · · · · · · · · · · · · · · · · · · · · · · · · · · · · · · · ·

# Exercise 3.8 ✏

Copy these adverbs and next to each one write the adjective from which it was formed.

1. naughtily
2. confidently
3. abruptly
4. cheekily
5. stoically

· · · · · · · · · · · · · · · · · · · · · · · · · · · · · · · · · · · · · · · · · · · · · · · · · ·

# Speaking and listening

1. Hot-seating: Take turns in sitting in the 'hot seat' (a chair at the front of the class) and answering questions from the class in rôle – either as the narrator, Laura, from *The Wreck of the Zanzibar*, or as one of the divers on the *Mary Rose* project. Try to answer others' questions as though you really are the person you claim to be.

2. Look again at the passage from *The Wreck of the Zanzibar*. Form groups of about five and imagine you are the crew hauling the gig to rescue the shipwrecked sailors. When the waves capsize the boat everyone wants to give up apart from the Chief who urges everyone on to Rushy Bay. Play out this scene together.

3. Imagine you are a newspaper reporter. You have been sent to interview one of the divers who found the bowcastle from the *Mary Rose*. Write this interview, setting out your questions for the diver and the answers he (or she) might give you. You will need to find out as much information as you can for your readers.

4.  Work with a partner. Take turns in imagining you have found a special object at the bottom of the ocean. Your partner must guess what the object is by asking up to twenty questions to which the answers may be only 'yes' or 'no'.

# Have you read?

The following stories and non-fiction titles involve finding treasures beneath the sea.

*Shipwreck on the Pirate Islands* by Geronimo Stilton (Scholastic Paperbacks)
*Dive England's Greatest Wrecks* by Rod Macdonald (Mainstream Publishing)
*The Treasure Seekers* by Edith Nesbit, narrated by Teresa Gallagher (Naxos Audiobooks)
*Adventure Double: 'Amazon Adventure' and 'Diving Adventure'* by Willard Price (Red Fox)
*Raising the Dead: The Skeleton Crew of King Henry VIII's Great Ship the Mary Rose* by A. J. Stirland (John Wiley and Sons Ltd.)
*Treasure Island: From the story by Robert Louis Stevenson* by Angela Wilkes (ed) (Usborne Publishing Ltd.)
*Treasure Island* narrated by Jasper Britton (Naxos Audiobooks)
*The Cave Divers* by Robert F. Burgess (Aqua Press)
*Diving the World* by Ken McAlpine (Hugh Lauter Levin Associates)

# Other things to do...

*   Find out more about the famous Tudor ship, *Mary Rose*. You may be surprised to discover whose flagship it was! You can find plenty of information in library books, or you may like to look at the following websites:
    www.historicdockyard.co.uk
    www.bbc.co.uk/history
    www.maryrose.org
    www.royal-navy.mod.uk

- In *The Wreck of the Zanzibar* news of the shipwreck travels quickly around the island. But if there had been a newspaper in print at the time, what might it have said? Design and print a front page for a newspaper, in which the story of the shipwreck is run as headline news. Think of a good headline and remember to include eyewitness accounts of what happened.

- Design and write the front page of a school newspaper. What will you call it? How much will it cost? What will the main headline be? Look at real newspapers to get an idea how their front pages are laid out. You may choose to design your own front page on a computer or write it out by hand.

# Chapter 4

## Time travelling

Have you ever wished time would speed up?  Or perhaps, when you have been enjoying yourself, have you wanted time to slow down a little?  But what if you could actually time travel – fly through space and time to visit your future or your past?  In the following passage Meg does just that.  Along with her brother, Charles, and their friend, Calvin, she encounters her first 'time wrinkle'.

Did the shadow fall across the moon or did the moon simply go out, extinguished as abruptly and completely as a candle?  There was still the sound of leaves, a terrified, terrifying rushing.  All light was gone.  Darkness was complete.  Suddenly the wind was gone, and all sound.  Meg felt that
5 Calvin was being torn from her.  When she reached for him her fingers touched nothing.

She screamed out, 'Charles!' and whether it was to help him or for him to help her, she did not know.  The word was flung back down her throat and she choked on it.

10 She was completely alone.

She had lost the protection of Calvin's hand.  Charles was nowhere, either to save or to turn to.  She was alone in a fragment of nothingness.  No light, no sound, no feeling.  Where was her body?  She tried to move in her panic, but there was nothing to move.  Just as light and sound had vanished,
15 she was gone, too.  The corporeal Meg simply was not.

Then she felt her limbs again.  Her legs and arms were tingling faintly, as though they had been asleep.  She blinked her eyes rapidly, but though she herself was somehow back, nothing else was.  It was not as simple as darkness, or absence of light.  Darkness has a tangible quality; it can be
20 moved through and felt; in darkness you can bark your shins; the world of things still exists around you.  She was lost in a horrifying void.

It was the same way with the silence.  This was more than silence.  A deaf person can feel vibrations.  Here there was nothing to feel.

Suddenly she was aware of her heart beating rapidly within the cage of
25 her ribs.  Had it stopped before?  What had made it start again?  The

tingling in her arms and legs grew stronger, and suddenly she felt movement. This movement, she felt, must be the turning of
30   the earth, rotating on its axis, travelling its elliptic course about the sun. And this feeling of moving with the earth was somewhat like the feeling of
35   being in the ocean, out in the ocean beyond the rising and falling of the breakers, lying on the moving water, pulsing gently with the swells, and feeling the
40   gentle, inexorable tug of the moon.

I am asleep; I am dreaming, she thought. I'm having a nightmare. I want to wake up. Let me wake up.

'Well!' Charles Wallace's voice said. 'That was quite a trip! I do think you might have warned us.'

45   Light began to pulse and quiver. Meg blinked and shoved shakily at her glasses and there was Charles Wallace standing indignantly in front of her, his hands on his hips. 'Meg!' he shouted. 'Calvin! Where are you?'

She saw Charles, she heard him, but she could not go to him. She could not shove through the strange, trembling light to meet him.

50   Calvin's voice came as though it were pushing through a cloud. 'Well, just give me time, will you? I'm older than you are.'

Meg gasped. It wasn't that Calvin wasn't there and then that he was. It wasn't that part of him came first and then the rest of him followed, like a hand and then an arm, an eye and then a nose. It was a sort of
55   shimmering, a looking at Calvin through water, through smoke, through fire, and then there he was, solid and reassuring.

*(From A Wrinkle in Time by Madeleine L'Engle, 1962)*

# Exercise 4.1 ✏️

Answer the following questions using complete sentences.

1. In the story Charles, Meg and Calvin are sitting in an orchard when their strange experience begins. Find a word or phrase in the first paragraph that shows this.

2. Write three words of your own to describe what 'nothingness' feels like.

3. Why does Meg call out Charles's name? Give two reasons.

4. Why do you think the author has written the sentence 'She was completely alone' as a separate paragraph? What effect does this have?

5. Why do you think Meg describes her experience as a 'nightmare'? (line 41)

6. Use a dictionary to find and write definitions of the following words:

   (a) extinguished (line 2); (b) fragment (line 12); (c) corporeal (line 15); (d) void (line 21).

. . . . . . . . . . . . . . . . . . . . . . . . . . . . . . . . . . . . . . . . . .

## What is time?

Today we can keep track of time by glancing at a wristwatch or looking at a clock, but it was not always so easy. Here are some frequently asked questions about time from the website of the famous Royal Observatory in Greenwich – where time has been carefully observed for centuries.

5   How can I tell if my watch is telling the right time?
You could compare your watch with a friend's. If they both say the same, you could check with another friend just to make sure. If the different watches show different times, you could check them by listening to the Greenwich time signal on the radio. At certain times of the day, usually on
10   the hour, six pips are broadcast in quick succession. The last pip sounds slightly different from the rest. If your minute and second hand are both on the twelve when the last pip starts, then your watch is telling the right time.

But how do they know when to broadcast the six pips?
The pips are controlled by the time service at the BBC. Nowadays the
15   time of transmission is worked out by comparing the time shown on more than 200 extremely accurate atomic clocks in different parts of the world.

In the past, however, the clocks at the Greenwich observatory were used to work out when to transmit the pips.

But how did they know that the Greenwich clocks were right? The astronomers at Greenwich used the stars to check the accuracy of their clocks. Each day the earth spins once on its axis, and because of this we see the sun seeming to move across the sky. It rises higher during the morning and sinks lower during the afternoon. The sun is only one of many stars which we see moving in this way. From their records, the astronomers were able to predict when each of the brightest stars would reach its highest point, and this gave them a reliable means of checking their clocks.

Does it matter how accurate our clocks and watches are? To catch the start of a television programme, or a particular train, then you do need to know the time fairly accurately. Two hundred years ago, before there were trains and televisions, most people didn't need to know the time so precisely. People who worked in factories were usually woken by 'knocker-uppers' who went from house to house with long poles knocking on the windows.

When was the first clock made? Until the 13th century, there were no mechanical clocks as we know them. The oldest mechanical clock in England that still exists is the Salisbury Cathedral clock. It was made in 1386, and is still in the cathedral today. The second oldest clock can be seen working in the Science Museum, and was made for Wells Cathedral in 1392. Like other early clocks it does not have a face or hands, but tells the time by striking each quarter hour. Before mechanical clocks, people relied on other types of clocks such as sundials and water clocks.

*(Source www.nmm.ac.uk © National Maritime Museum, Greenwich)*

# Exercise 4.2

Answer the following questions using complete sentences.

1. What is the best way of checking that your watch is accurate?

2. How did the astronomers at Greenwich check the accuracy of their clocks?

3. What exactly are the BBC's 'pips'?

4. Without face or hands, how did some of the earliest mechanical clocks tell the time?

5. Describe, in a sentence or two, why keeping a close track of the time may be more important to us today than it was to our ancestors.

6. Use a dictionary to find the meanings of the following words:
   (a) *transmission* (line 15); (b) *succession* (line 10); (c) *astronomer* (line 23); (d) *predict* (line 33).

# Exercise 4.3

Your turn to write:

1. What must it feel like to travel through time? Look again at Meg's strange experience in the passage above. Do you think this is realistic? Write about an imaginary time-travelling journey of your own. What will happen to you? What will you see? How will it feel? Try to make your description as vivid as possible.

2. Re-read the extract from *A Wrinkle in Time* and then continue the story in any way you think is appropriate. Where are they? What is the date? Describe the landscape in front of them. Will they be able to return to their own time?

3. Have you heard the phrase 'Time flies when you're having fun'? Have you ever enjoyed something so much that you lost track of time? Why do the bad times in life drag on and the good moments seem to zoom by? Write about a time when you were enjoying yourself so much you wished time could 'stand still'.

4.  If you had all the time in the world, with no school and no prep to complete, what would you do? Write about how you would spend your time if you never had to work again. Would you waste precious time? Would you become bored?

. . . . . . . . . . . . . . . . . . . . . . . . . . . . . . . . . . . . . . . . . . . . . . .

# Learning about language

## Verbs

Sometimes known as 'doing words', **verbs** tell us what the subject of a sentence is *doing*. They show us the action that is taking place.

*Henry* **bought** *a new watch today.*

Every sentence needs at least one verb for it to make sense. Some sentences can have many verbs in them.

*After they had* **watched** *the match, Jane and her father* **bought** *ice creams and* **sat** *and* **ate** *them in the park.*

The **tense** of a verb tells you whether the action is taking place in the **present**, took place in the **past** or will happen in the **future**. This is discussed in more detail in *Can you spell?* below.

. . . . . . . . . . . . . . . . . . . . . . . . . . . . . . . . . . . . . . . . . . . . . . .

# Exercise 4.4

Copy the following passage and underline every verb. The first three have been done for you.

The astronomers at Greenwich <u>used</u> the stars to <u>check</u> the accuracy of their clocks. Each day the earth <u>spins</u> once on its axis, and because of this we see the sun seeming to move across the sky. It rises higher during the morning and sinks lower during the afternoon. The sun is only one of many stars which we see moving in this way. From their records, the astronomers were able to predict when each of the brightest stars would reach its highest point, and this gave them a reliable means of checking their clocks.

# Exercise 4.5 🖊

Always try to use interesting verbs whenever you can – they make your writing leap from the page and dazzle your readers. Why not use *galloped* instead of *ran* for example, or *leapt* instead of *jumped*?

Here are some interesting verbs. Write a suitable sentence for each one. The first has been done for you.

1. crunched: *The fallen leaves and twigs <u>crunched</u> beneath our feet as we walked through the forest.*

2. fumbled

3. trickled

4. dashed

5. trudged

6. wailed

## Commas

The comma (,) is an extremely useful tool. It enables us to put lots of different pieces of information into the same sentence without confusing the reader.

A comma can be especially useful when we want to make a list of different things. For example:

*My new car has electric windows, satellite navigation, central locking and air conditioning.*

*'Can I have a white loaf, three doughnuts, four sausage rolls and a gingerbread man, please?'*

Notice how the final item in each list does not have a comma before it, but an 'and' instead. This rounds off the list and tells the reader that the end is in sight. The word 'or' can sometimes be used in the same way.

*What shall we have on the barbeque: chicken wings, lamb kebabs, beef burgers* **or** *sausages?*

# Exercise 4.6 ✏

The following sentences all have lists in them. Copy out each one, inserting commas wherever you think they are needed.

1. This morning I had English French Geography and Music.

2. Will the following boys please report to my office: James Santosh Peter and Simon.

3. At the greengrocer's shop I bought a cauliflower some beans a melon and a bag of potatoes.

4. Since buying the motor-caravan Grandpa and I have been to Somerset Devon Suffolk and North Yorkshire.

5. On the menu today we have a choice of lasagna shepherd's pie curry or salmon.

Commas are also useful when we want to use more than one adjective to describe a noun, or several adverbs to describe a verb.

*The soft, silky sand stretched out towards the warm, welcoming, tropical seas.*

*Slowly, steadily, and without a sound, the shadows drew closer.*

There are many other uses for commas. You will learn plenty more about them in the next book in this course, SYRWTL English Book 1.

. . . . . . . . . . . . . . . . . . . . . . . . . . . . . . . . . . . . . . . . . . . . . . . . . .

# Exercise 4.7 ✏

Copy the following sentences, putting a comma wherever you think it is required.

1. Bravely confidently and with no sign of wobbling Molly rode her new bicycle.

2. The dark lonely and mysterious forest looked unwelcoming to the traveller.

3. After a long day at work Michael was looking forward to a long hot and relaxing bath.

4. The music examiner said the student had played confidently accurately and with lots of feeling.

5. The climb to the summit was painful dangerous and very long.

# Can you spell?

## Verb endings: past tense

Most stories – though not all – are written in the past tense.
This means the verbs show actions that happened in the past. For example:

*The alien <u>watched</u> as the spaceship <u>landed</u> safely on his planet.*

The letters '-ed' have been added to the verbs *to watch* and *to land* to show that these actions happened in the past. These verbs each have a 'regular' past tense.

However, some verbs have an 'irregular' past tense.
Look at the following:

*to swim – I swam*          *to eat – I ate*

*to ride – I rode*          *to lead – I led*

Have you ever heard anyone say 'I swimmed' or 'I eated', or 'I rided'? And misspelling the past tense of 'I lead' is a very common mistake: it is 'I led' (with no 'a'). Verbs that have an irregular past tense just have to be learnt when you meet them. There are no rules: that's why we say they are irregular!

. . . . . . . . . . . . . . . . . . . . . . . . . . . . . . . . . . . . . . . . . . . . . . . .

# Exercise 4.8

Copy out the following grid and see if you can fill in the missing words. The first line has been completed for you. Remember: some words may simply require '-ed', but others may be irregular.

| Verb | Past tense |
|------|------------|
| to start | I started |
| to sing | ? |
| ? | I wrote |
| to wish | ? |
| ? | I swept |
| to look | ? |
| to read | ? |
| ? | I drove |
| to find | ? |
| ? | I arrived |

# Speaking and listening

1.  In a group of three or four, make a list of the different ways in which you choose to spend your spare time. Do you have similar hobbies, or do you each have very different interests? Once you have made your list, share them among the whole class. Make a chart of the most popular ways to fill your free time.

2.  Have you ever noticed how we refer to clocks as having hands and a face? In pairs, take turns in using your hands and face to tell the time. One person can be the clock, while the other positions the hands to show different times on a clock face. Once you have practised for a while, strike different times with your hands and your partner must guess the correct time.

3.  If you could travel back in time to visit any period of history, which would you choose? Write a short piece explaining when you would choose and why. Do you think you might visit the Ancient Egyptians or have tea with Henry VIII?

4.  Just a minute! Could you keep talking on a given subject for a whole minute? Take turns in class at speaking for a minute on a subject chosen by another, without hesitating, deviating or repeating yourself. You might agree to ban that awful word 'erm' too.

# Have you read?

The following stories and non-fiction titles explore the theme of 'time'.

*Horrid Henry and the Mega-mean Time Machine: Book 13* by Francesca Simon (Orion Children's Books)
*The Time Machine (Fast Track Classics)* abridged from the classic novel by H. G. Wells (Evans Brothers – Books for Children)
*Molly Moon's Hypnotic Time Travel Adventure* by Georgia Byng (HarperCollins)
*Thief of Time (A Discworld Novel)* by Terry Pratchett (Corgi Adult)
*The Wheel of Time Series* by Robert Jordan (Orbit)
*The Time Travelling Cat and the Roman Eagle* by Julia Jarman (Andersen Press)

*Time Spinner* by Roy Apps (Andersen Press)
*Time Swing* by Pippa Goodhart (Mammoth)
*The New Policeman* by Kate Thompson (Random House)
*The Encyclopaedia of Science Fiction* edited by Peter Nicholls
and John Clute (Orbit)

. . . . . . . . . . . . . . . . . . . . . . . . . . . . . . . . . . . . . . . . . . . . . . . . . .

# Other things to do...

- Write a rhyming poem that uses lots of homophones (Chapter 1, page 10). Try to place the homophones at the end of each line. You may like to use rhyming couplets or place the matching homophones on alternate lines to create an 'a-b-a-b' effect. See if you can learn the words of your poem by heart and then perform it to the class.

- Find out more about the Royal Observatory in Greenwich. It really is a fascinating place. You could try to make a special visit with your family or consult these websites: www.rog.nmm.ac.uk and www.greenwich-guide. org.uk.

- How familiar are you with time? Could you identify when ten seconds have passed, or half a minute, or two minutes? Work with a partner and see if you can accurately identify how long a minute really is. You may find it is longer than you thought (but, of course, it depends on whether you are having fun).

# Chapter 5

## Back of the net

Mal Peet's story is not your average footballer's tale. The Keeper may not be what you expected. Read the extract below and then see if you can find the book for yourself. It will certainly surprise you.

I knew every inch of the path, of course, and all its tricks – the places where it hid itself, pretended to fade away, the places where the forest stretched its fingers out to lash at your eyes, where roots snaked out to trip you up. But I had never gone in there at night before, and I had never
5   run so desperately towards the clearing. Here and there tiny splashes of silver light lay on the forest floor like coins, and now and again I caught a glimpse of the fat-faced moon sliding through the canopy of branches way above me.

I was shaking, and soaked with sweat, when I stumbled into the clearing. I
10  put my hands on my knees and dragged the air, always sharper and cleaner here, into my lungs. The clearing was drenched in cold light. The moon had come to a stop overhead. Everything was divided into just two colours: brilliant silver and an inky blue-black. The silence was like something solid you could lean against, and rest, and recover from miracles.

15  I did not expect the Keeper to be there. Whatever and whoever he was, he seemed to depend on daylight. I was quite sure he would not materialise at night. When my breathing had steadied, I straightened up.

He was standing in the goalmouth, his back against the right post, arms folded over his chest, staring at the ground. No football. My heart lurched
20  like a truck going over a rut in the road. It was as hard as it had ever been to walk towards him. I stopped at the penalty spot.

'It has happened, then,' he said. It was not a question. So I didn't answer.

He began to pace. He touched the upright nearest him, walked to the other, touched that, walked back, touched. Walked back. I waited. At last
25  he faced me.

'Because of what I am,' he said, 'I have almost forgotten what it is like to be afraid. I should have taught you more about fear.'

'I have signed for DSJ,' I said. 'Why are you talking about fear?  I am not afraid.  I am happy.  Do not spoil this, please.'

30 He looked at me.  From within the shadow of his face two tiny lights shone, like distant stars in deepest space.

I said, 'No, that's not true.  I am afraid.  I am afraid of not coming here.  I do not know what I will do without you.' I

35 was outraged to discover tears in my eyes.

The Keeper smiled. Actually smiled,

40 like a living person. Tiny muscles reorganized his face.  One more amazing thing to

45 happen on one amazing day.

*(From Keeper by Mal Peet)*

# Exercise 5.1 ✏

Answer these questions using full sentences.

1. What do you think the narrator means when he says 'the forest stretched its fingers out to lash at your eyes'? (lines 2–3)

2. Where is the silver light coming from?

3. In a few sentences, and using your own words as far as possible, describe the sights, sounds and the atmosphere of the wood on the night the narrator returns.

4. Why do you think the narrator was surprised to find the Keeper in the goalmouth?

5. Based on what you have read, who, or what, do you think the Keeper might be?

6. Write short definitions for the following words: (a) *canopy* (line 7); (b) *drenched* (line 11); (c) *materialise* (line 17); (d) *outraged* (line 35).

. . . . . . . . . . . . . . . . . . . . . . . . . . . . . . . . . . . . . . . . . . .

## Save of the century

This was the 1970 World Cup Final that everyone was dreaming of: the holders, England, against the favourites, Brazil. But instead of meeting in the final, the two nations met on 7th June in the group matches, in the 98-degree heat of Guadalajara. In the event, both teams went through to
5   the quarter-finals and might have met again in the final, but for the fact that England lost their quarter-final to West Germany (in the absence of first-choice goalkeeper Gordon Banks), while Brazil moved majestically through to the final and a legendary 4-1 win against Italy.

And so it is that many England fans think of 7th June as the 'real final'. Six
10   of the England squad that day had played in England's 1966 triumph at Wembley, four years earlier. Brazil fielded what is considered to be their best-ever side. It was going to be an epic contest. Epic, but low scoring – the only goal came 14 minutes into the second half, from Jairzinho, off a pass from Pele. But for England fans, the defining moment of that match
15   and of the entire campaign came 10 minutes into the goalless first half – That Save by Gordon Banks.

In the tenth minute, Pele, the acclaimed master of the header (and everything else), leapt for the ball from a perfect position and headed it downwards, towards Banks's right hand post. It was good, and Pele knew
20 it. Before it had even reached the net he began celebrating his goal. But Banks dived across the goalmouth and somehow managed to get a hand to it, pushing the ball up and over the crossbar for the save of the century – an exquisite moment that has passed into footballing folklore.

*(From Great Sporting Moments by Ian Harrison)*

# Exercise 5.2

Read the above passage from *Great Sporting Moments* and answer the following questions using full sentences.

1. What is the reason given for England losing their quarter-final match against West Germany?

2. Why do many England fans look back on this particular match as the 'real final' of the tournament?

3. How can we tell that Pele was expecting his shot to find the back of the net?

4. Who won the match in the end?

5. Use a dictionary to find out what the following words mean: (a) *majestically* (line 7); (b) *epic* (line 12); (c) *defining* (line 14); (d) *folklore* (line 23).

# Exercise 5.3 🖉

Your turn to write:

1. Imagine you are a sports journalist on a national newspaper. You are given the opportunity to interview Gordon Banks after the match in which he made that historic save. Write an account of the interview with Gordon. You can set it out as a series of questions and answers. Try to include his thoughts and feelings during and after the match.

2. Write a story about a great sporting moment – perhaps a crucial goal in a soccer or netball match, or an injury in a hockey match. Write as if you were there as the author has done in *The Keeper*. Remember to include as much description as you can to build excitement and suspense for the reader.

3. Produce a short piece of writing on the benefits of sport and why everyone should engage in some sort of physical activity. Persuade readers to get up and put their tracksuits on.

# Learning about language

## Adjectival phrases

As you know, an adjective is a **describing word** that describes the noun or pronoun it is accompanying. Look at the following examples, taken from the passages above.

| Adjective | Noun |
|-----------|------|
| silver | light |
| amazing | day |
| real | final |
| epic | contest |
| perfect | position |

Sometimes we may need more than one word to describe a noun in a sentence, so we use a group of words which act together like an adjective. Look at the following examples which also come from passages above:

| Adjectival phrase | Noun |
|---|---|
| one more amazing<br>fat-faced<br>inky blue-black<br>best-ever<br>goalless first | thing<br>moon<br>shadows<br>side<br>half |

These are called **adjectival phrases** because they are groups of words (phrases) doing the job of an adjective.

# Exercise 5.4

Now see if you can use these adjectival phrases in sentences of your own:

1. cool and refreshing

2. rusty old

3. kind and helpful

4. large white

5. with brown eyes

## Prepositions

A preposition is a word that tells us how two nouns (or pronouns) relate to each other. We might say it tells us the 'position' one thing has in relation to another. For example:

The ball fell **through** the keeper's hands.

The defender ran **after** the striker.

The captain fell **onto** his knees.

There are many common prepositions. There are two sorts:

Place prepositions:
around, across, below, above, beside, beyond, over, under, to, on

Time prepositions:
until, after, before, during, at, from, since, while, between, about

# Exercise 5.5 ✏

Rewrite the following sentences, changing the preposition each time for an alternative one in order to produce a different meaning.

1. The player walked <u>onto</u> the pitch.

2. The goalkeeper stood <u>beside</u> the goalpost.

3. 'We'll meet <u>before</u> the match for a drink.'

4. 'Walk <u>under</u> the bridge and you'll reach the stadium.'

5. The ball disappeared <u>over</u> the bushes.

# Exercise 5.6 ✏

Write a sentence of your own using each of the following prepositions:

behind       until          near           amid           before

# Can you spell?

## Comparative and superlative endings

Sports commentators often exaggerate when they are describing great sporting events, historic matches or talented sports players. They will often use phrases like:

*the greatest footballer*        *the strongest runner*

*the biggest challenge*          *the happiest moment*

*the liveliest crowd*            *the cleverest cricketer*

In each case, the commentators are using the **superlative** form of adjectives. Can you recognise what the original adjectives were?   For example:

*biggest* comes from *big*        *greatest* comes from *great*        and so on.

But it does not end there.  Between 'great' and 'greatest' there lies 'greater', which is the **comparative** form of the adjective.  Here we can use the **comparative** and **superlative** forms of the original adjective to show different degrees of greatness.

Here is another example:

*tall* –          *tall**er*** –          *tall**est***

**adjective     comparative     superlative**

. . . . . . . . . . . . . . . . . . . . . . . . . . . . . . .

# Exercise 5.7

Copy the following adjectives and put their comparative and superlative forms next to each one.

1. small

2. high

3. rich

4. keen

5. bright

For most comparatives we add '–er' to the original adjective (or root word). For most superlatives we usually add '–est'. But as is so often the case with this complicated language of ours, there are plenty of exceptions to this rule. Look at the following examples:

easy – easier – easiest

hot – hotter – hottest

important – more important – most important

In the first example we must change the 'y' to an 'i' before adding the usual comparative and superlative endings of '–er' and '–est'.

In the second we need to double the last letter 't' before adding the same endings.

In the third, the entire rule changes. Think how strange the words 'importanter' or 'importantest' would sound. Instead, we must add the words *more* and *most* to enable us to show different degrees of importance. This is what usually happens when the root word has two or more syllables.

# Exercise 5.8 ✏

Copy the following grid and then fill in all the missing adjectives, comparatives and superlatives. Remember to watch out for those unusual spelling changes.

| Adjective | Comparative | Superlative |
| --- | --- | --- |
| pretty | | |
| | more beautiful | |
| | | sunniest |
| sad | | |
| | more gracious | |
| | | busiest |

And, of course, it does not end there! Some adjectives change completely when we need to show their comparative and superlative forms:

bad – worse – worst

little – less – least

Can you think of the comparative and superlative forms of these words?

good

many

• • • • • • • • • • • • • • • • • • • • • • • • • • • • • • • • • • • • • • • •

# Speaking and listening

1. Find a partner to work with. Re-read the extract from *The Keeper* together. This is a mysterious story raising many questions for the reader. Share the sort of questions that occur to you as you read the passage – for example, *Who is the Keeper? Why is he in the woods? Who, or what, is DSJ?* Share your own opinions in answer to these questions and listen carefully to the views of your partner.

2. Get into groups of three or four. Share stories about memorable soccer or netball matches you have played in. What was memorable about them? Did you score a goal? Did you suffer an injury? After a few minutes report back to the class, speaking on behalf of a friend in the group. Be sure to tell his or her story as accurately as you can.

3. Imagine you are a sports reporter for a news programme on television. With a friend, act out a post-match interview with Gordon Banks in which he shares his thoughts about 'that save'. Practise your interview several times and then perform it for your class.

## Have you read?

The following stories all involve a sport of some kind.

*Sport (A Harriet the Spy Adventure)* by Louise Fitzhugh (Delacote Press)
*Sport Stories You'll Have a Ball With* by K. Kessler (Sagebrush)
*Superstar Coach:1* by Thomas Taylor (Sport Story Publishers)
*Abbey the Bad Sport* by Ann M. Martin (Apple)
*Football Mad No.4* by Paul Stewart (Scholastic)
*Soccer at Sandford* by Rob Childs (Yearling Books)

Here are some interesting autobiographies of famous sporting heroes.

*My Grand Slam Year* by Gavin Henson (Harper Sport)
*Race Against Time* by Ellen MacArthur (Michael Joseph Ltd.)
*Opening Up: My Autobiography* by Mike Atherton (Coronet Books)
*Black, White and Gold* by Kelly Holmes (Virgin Books)
*Martin Johnson Autobiography* by Martin Johnson (Headline Book Publishing Ltd.)
*My Side – The Autobiography* by David Beckham (Harper Collins Willow)

# Other things to do...

- Write your own sports match report to describe a game you have played recently at school or in a weekend team. Try to build plenty of suspense into your writing. Talk about the reactions of the crowd and the expressions on the players' faces when a goal is scored or a penalty is missed.

- Choose a particular sport – netball, hockey or soccer for example – and find out more about how it first began. Where and when was the first match played? How have the rules changed over the years? How popular is the sport today? You can find information on websites, CD ROMs and from sporting encyclopaedias.

- Do you have any sporting heroes of your own? Who are they? Why do you admire them so much? Choose one such hero and find out more about him or her. When did he or she begin playing the sport? How did he or she start? In what ways do you think you might be like him or her?

# Chapter 6

### The boy who fell out of the sky

The story of Daedalus and Icarus is very famous. Like many other Greek myths and legends, it leaves us with a moral, or lesson, to learn. What do you think is the moral of this story?

'You know you've always wanted to fly?' Daedalus said. 'Well, now's your chance.'

Daedalus went over to a large box in the corner of the room. Somehow, Daedalus had always known that one day, he and Icarus might have to
5   escape from Crete. So he had made wings from bird feathers, and set aside four balls of wax with which to fix them.

Daedalus lifted the wings from the box and worked quickly to attach the smaller pair on to Icarus's back.

'Poor Icarus,' Daedalus thought, 'he believes it's all a game.'

10   At last, Daedalus was satisfied with Icarus's wings. They were well fixed and should carry him safely across the sea. However, as Daedalus fixed his own larger wings on to his own back, he had a strong warning for Icarus.

'Remember your wings are stuck on with wax,' Daedalus said. 'Wax melts in heat, so take care not to fly too near the Sun, or your wings will fall off!
15   You understand, don't you Icarus?'

'Oh yes, father, of course I understand,' Icarus replied, only half-listening.

Icarus was too excited at the thought of flying like a bird to think of anything else. The wings on his back were made of beautiful snow-white feathers, just like those of the birds he had often watched flying over the
20   island.

Daedalus looked at the eager excited face of his young son and prayed that no harm would befall him.

'Just follow me,' he told Icarus. 'Don't fly any higher than I do, and you will be all right!'

25   Just then Daedalus heard a sound in the corridor outside. It was the tramp, tramp, tramp of soldiers' feet marching speedily towards his rooms.

'Quickly, Icarus!' Daedalus spoke urgently, as he led his son on to the balcony. 'Jump up into the air when I tell you, and don't look down!' Daedalus gave Icarus a quick anxious kiss, then said: 'Now, Icarus! Jump!'

30 Icarus did as he was told and together with his father, he rose slowly into the air. The wings attached to his back moved up and down, and before long, Icarus and Daedalus were flying high above the grounds of the palace, over the golden sandy beaches along the shore and out to sea. The Sun shone warm and bright all around them, the sea below sparkled and the
35 air felt fresh and clean on their faces as they flew along. Every now and then, Daedalus looked round anxiously, to ensure Icarus was behind him. Every time, Icarus waved excitedly at his father. He was enjoying himself.

Icarus decided to try something. He glanced ahead to see that his father was not looking, then spread his wings out straight. He waggled them a
40 little at the tips and found himself flying sideways.

'It works!' Icarus cried, greatly thrilled.

Next, Icarus leaned downwards and swooped for a second or two, then zoomed upwards again so that he was once more flying behind Daedalus. Icarus could almost believe now that he had never been anything but a
45 flying creature.

Just then, a flock of birds came zooming up, right in front of Icarus. They were making for greater heights, before levelling out again. Icarus followed them. Up, up he went, hardly noticing that it was becoming hotter and hotter as he got higher and higher. The Sun was shining more and more
50 brightly, but Icarus did not stop.

'I can fly as high as the birds,' he said. 'I know I can.'

Suddenly, far below, Daedalus turned round again. He found the sky behind him was empty. Greatly alarmed, Daedalus looked up and saw, to his horror, that Icarus was nothing but a small dot high in the sky.

55 'Icarus! Icarus!' Daedalus cried out in great fear. 'Icarus, come back!'

Icarus was far too high to hear him. Besides, he was feeling rather faint from the heat of the Sun. He also grew more and more frightened as the wind currents took hold of him and shot him upwards at tremendous speed. Then, without warning, Icarus felt two burning patches on his back.

60 The wax! It was melting! Suddenly, instead of flying, Icarus was falling. Below him as he fell, he saw his two wings being thrown about by the wind. They had come off.

Down, down Icarus plunged, faster and faster. Daedalus was turning this way and that, trying to see where his son was. Suddenly, the boy fell past
65 him, arms flailing wildly, hands trying to clutch at the air. Daedalus went cold with fear and grief. He was helpless. All he could do was to watch Icarus falling away from him, getting smaller and smaller until a splash of foam in the sea below marked the spot where he plunged into the water.

'Icarus, my son, my son!' Daedalus moaned. A dreadful ache entered his
70 heart, for he realised the boy could not have survived such a long fall into the sea.

*(From Myths and Legends by
Brenda Ralph Lewis)*

# Exercise 6.1 ✏️

Answer the following questions in complete sentences.

1. In the passage, we learn that Daedalus had always known he might one day have to escape from Crete. How had he prepared for this?

2. Explain, in your own words as far as possible, the warning Daedalus gives to his son.

3. Why do you think the author has used the phrase 'snow-white' to describe the feathers? What effect does it have on the reader?

4. Replace the word 'cried' in line 41 with an alternative, keeping the same meaning as far as you can.

5. Why should Icarus believe that 'he had never been anything but a flying creature'? What made him think in this way?

6. In a few lines, explain the lessons we might learn from Icarus's mistakes.

· · · · · · · · · · · · · · · · · · · · · · · · · · · · · · · · · · · · · · · · · · · · · · · · · · · ·

## Fly like a bird

Since the days of the mythical birdman Daedalus in ancient Greece, people have longed to fly like the birds. For centuries, some believed that if they could mimic the birds and their flapping wings, they too would be able to fly. In the Middle Ages in Europe, many a reckless experimenter strapped
5  on wings and lunged into the air from towers and cliff tops – only to plummet to the ground, often fatally. Then, in the 15th century, the brilliant Italian artist and thinker Leonardo da Vinci applied his mind to unlocking the secrets of flight. Leonardo too believed that people could learn from the birds how to fly. But he realised that human arms are too weak to
10  flap wings for long, so he sketched designs for flapping wing machines or 'ornithopters'. Centuries later, these sketches were discovered in his notebooks. As far as we know, Leonardo never tried to build his machines and sadly, they would never have flown; imitating bird flight is far more complicated than even Leonardo understood. But his ideas may be one of
15  the earliest scientific attempts to invent a flying machine.

Wings are lifted by the air flowing above and beneath as they cut through the air. Air pushed over the top speeds up and is stretched out, so that the pressure here drops. But air flowing beneath slows down and pressure rises. So, in effect, the wing is sucked from above and pushed

20  from below. Even a flat board can give some lift, but pioneers like Lilienthal discovered that a curved or 'cambered' surface is best. Today, wings are thicker and far more effective than those of the pioneers. Research with computers and wind tunnels ensures the right shape for each type of aircraft.

*(Flying Machine by Andrew Nahum)*

# Exercise 6.2

Answer the following questions in complete sentences.

1.  According to some people many years ago what did you need to do in order to be able to fly?

2.  Were these early attempts to fly successful? What happened?

3.  What do you think is meant by the phrase 'unlocking the secrets of flight'?

4.  In the passage we learn how wings actually work. Draw and label a diagram to show how a wing works. Refer to the explanation in the passage and rewrite this information in labels and captions.

5.  Use a dictionary to find definitions for the following words: (a) *mythical* (line 1); (b) *mimic* (line 3); (c) *plummet* (line 6); (d) *pioneers* (line 20).

# Exercise 6.3

Your turn to write:

1.  Re-read the story of Daedalus and Icarus. Picture it as a scene in a play. Think about the setting, the characters and the dialogue. Rewrite the passage as a playscript. Whenever a character speaks, put his name in the margin and write the words he actually says. The story narration and description will need to be rewritten as stage directions.

2. Put yourself in Icarus's shoes. Imagine you are flying through the air like a bird with the magnificent wings your father has made for you. Record how you feel in a poem or descriptive prose. Describe the feeling of the wind in your face as you soar higher and higher in the sky towards the burning sun. You feel as light as a feather – as free as a bird.

3. Write a story of your own in which an inventor surprises his friends and actually makes a set of wings that enables him to fly just like a bird. Describe how the inventor struggles to persuade people around him that it *can* be done – then describe his first flight. Where does he fly to? What happens along the way? Does he become famous?

4. What will aeroplanes look like in the future? Do you think we shall eventually be flying to school and to the shops in the same way that we drive there today? How have aeroplanes changed our lives? How will they continue to change the way we live in years to come? Write a short essay in which you share your views.

# Learning about language

## Simple sentences

Read the following sentences, taken from the story of Daedalus and Icarus:

*He was enjoying himself.*        *Icarus decided to try something.*

These are **simple** sentences: they each contain a **subject** and a **predicate** (containing the **verb**). Simple sentences make sense on their own without any need for conjunctions, colons or semi-colons. They give us simple statements or ideas.

Simple sentences may seem rather plain, but they can be very useful for building tension in story writing. A small sentence can have a big impact on the reader. Look at the example below:

*Suddenly, instead of flying, Icarus was falling. Below him as he fell, he saw his two wings being thrown about by the wind. They had come off.*

The news that Icarus's wings have fallen off comes as quite a shock to the reader, especially when it is told in such direct terms. Here is another example on a different theme:

*After much deliberation, Josie and Emma at last decided to climb the great stone steps up to the ghost tower. When they reached the top, the wind rattled at the windows and the floorboards creaked beneath their feet. Suddenly the door slammed shut. They were locked in.*

Simple sentences can make our hearts speed up and our spines tingle!

· · · · · · · · · · · · · · · · · · · · · · · · · · · · · · · · · · · · · · · · · · · · · · · · · ·

# Exercise 6.4 ✐

Copy the following simple sentences, each time underlining the **subject** in one colour and the **verb** in another.

1. Daedalus strapped the wings to his son.

2. Icarus ignored his father's advice.

3. The wax melted.

4. Icarus plunged towards the sea.

5. Daedalus watched helplessly.

## Compound sentences

Look at the following sentences taken from the Daedalus story:

*Daedalus lifted the wings from the box and worked quickly to attach the smaller pair on to Icarus's back.*

*Daedalus looked at the eager excited face of his young son and prayed that no harm would befall him.*

These are **compound** sentences. A compound sentence is formed by joining two or more simple sentences together using a word such as *and, or* or *but*. Whereas simple sentences give us one statement or idea, compound sentences will give us two or more pieces of information, e.g.:

Simple: *I went shopping today. I bought a new tennis racket.*

Compound: *I went shopping today and bought a new tennis racket.*

Simple: *It was raining this morning. Now it is fine.*

Compound: *It was raining this morning but now it is fine.*

Compound sentences always have more than one verb and sometimes more than one subject too, e.g.:

| I | made | the cake and | Josie | iced | it. |
|---|---|---|---|---|---|
| *subject* | *verb* | | *subject* | *verb* | |

The word used to join two simple sentences to make a compound sentence is a **conjunction**.

## Conjunctions

Sometimes known as joining words, conjunctions link phrases or simple sentences together. The most common conjunctions are: **and, or** and **but**.

For example:

I went to the zoo <u>and</u> saw a zebra today.

Would you like to eat now <u>or</u> shall we wait a little longer?

We would have come sooner <u>but</u> we lost our way.

Other conjunctions include: **because   although   before   since   so than   that**

. . . . . . . . . . . . . . . . . . . . . . . . . . . . . . . . . . . . . . . . . . . .

# Exercise 6.5

Copy the following compound sentences and fill the gaps with one of these conjunctions: *and    but    or*

1.  Daedalus and his son jumped off the balcony _____ began to fly.

2.  The soldiers were after Daedalus and Icarus _____ they were able to escape.

3.  Daedalus warned his son not to fly too high _____ he wouldn't listen.

4.  Today you can fly in an aeroplane _____ you can take a ride in a hot air balloon.

5.  Many people have tried to fly by strapping wings to their arms _____ no one has ever managed it.

# Exercise 6.6

Insert one of the following conjunctions into these sentences.

*unless   after   because   that   but*

1. James said he would like to come _____ he may be a little late.

2. Gran knew who had eaten the cake _____ she saw the crumbs around my mouth.

3. The bride was late _____ the wedding car broke down.

4. The manager told his team _____ they could win the match if they really tried.

5. You had better avoid the prawns _____ you want to have a stomach ache.

# Exercise 6.7

Write a sentence of your own using each of the following conjunctions:

1. and

2. although

3. that

4. because

5. so

## Final word...

Conjunctions belong to a larger family of words known as **connectives**, which includes other types of joining words.

# Can you spell?

## Greek prefixes

Myths and legends like the story of Daedalus are not the only thing for which the Ancient Greeks are remembered. Did you know, for example, that many of the words we use today have their origins in the language of Ancient Greece?

Many prefixes (word beginnings) stem from Greek words. For example, the prefix, *anti-* is an Ancient Greek word meaning 'against', and so today we have words like:

**anti**freeze – liquid used in the radiator of motor cars to prevent freezing;

**anti**septic – relating to ointment that prevents a cut going septic;

**anti**social – behaviour that is not sociable and is offensive to others.

Similarly, the prefix, *mono-* is from the Greek word *monos* meaning 'alone', and so we have words like:

**mono**logue – a speech by one actor in a play;

**mono**cycle – a cycle with a single wheel used by acrobats (also known as a unicycle);

**mono**cle – a single eyeglass or lens.

# Exercise 6.8 ✏

Copy the following table which shows some common prefixes and the Greek words they stem from. Use a large dictionary to find out the original Greek meanings and then think of words we use today that have similar letters and meanings. The first line has been done for you.

| Prefix | Greek word | Greek meaning | English words |
|--------|-----------|---------------|---------------|
| mega- | megas | great | megastore |
| micro- | mikros | | |
| geo- | ge | | |
| poly- | polus | | |
| octa- | okto | | |

## Latin words

The Ancient Greeks are not the only people we should thank for giving us so many of our prefixes. Many other words we use today have their origins in Latin – around 50% of our language, in fact. So learning Latin at school really can help to improve your English.

Latin is a rich and fascinating language – and one that is still important in many professions today. Lawyers, scientists, doctors and historians all benefit from understanding some Latin.

Here are some Latin words and their meanings. Can you see how the related English words have been influenced by them?

| Latin word | Meaning | English words |
| --- | --- | --- |
| sequi | to follow | **sequ**ence |
| trans | across | **trans**atlantic, **trans**fer |
| uti | to use | **uti**lity, **uti**lise |
| videre | to see | **vide**o |
| duo | two | **duo**logue, **du**el |

# Exercise 6.9 ✏

Now copy and complete the following grid. Each time, write the Latin words and their meanings, and then find two related English words. Each time, look at the Latin word and see if it makes you think of a similar word we use today that might have a similar meaning.

| Latin word | Meaning | English words |
| --- | --- | --- |
| habitare | to live | |
| locus | place | |
| multi | many | |
| satis | enough | |
| quartus | fourth | |

# Speaking and listening

1. Hot-seating: Take turns to sit in the 'hot seat' at the front of the class and answer questions in the rôle of either Daedalus or Icarus. How did you feel when you first took to the air? Were you worried about the wax melting? Why did you ignore your father's advice?

2. Work with a partner. Imagine you are two of the soldiers who came for Daedalus and his son. Perform a short sketch in which you burst into their room and find that they have jumped over the balcony. You stand there, baffled by their disappearance, and then you see them flying like birds towards the horizon. Explain how you feel?

3. What is the lesson we can all learn from the mistakes Icarus makes? In a small group, discuss this question together and then share your views with the class. Is there a moral to this story? Can you think of a time in your own life when you have ignored the advice you have been given, only to regret it later?

4. Re-read the second passage in which an explanation is given for how a wing actually works. Read through the explanation and then cover it. Can you then explain to a friend, in your own words, howa wing works? See if you can repeat this without using your hands to help you. You will see how much we rely on gestures when we are explaining something.

# Have you read?

These stories involve well-known Greek myths.

*Greek Myths: Daedalus and Icarus* by Geraldine McCraughrean (Orchard Books)
*A Fall from the Sky: The Story of Daedalus and Icarus* by Ian Serraillier (Nelson)
*Wings* by Jane Yolen (Harcourt Children's Books)
*Black Ships Before Troy* by Rosemary Sutcliffe (et al) (Frances Lincoln Publishers)
*Illustrated Guide to Greek Myths and Legends* by C. Evans (et al)
(Usborne Publishing)
*Tales from the Greek Legends (Junior Classics)* by Edward Ferrie, narrated by Benjamin Soames (Naxos Audiobooks)

The following books contain interesting information about the history of flight.

*Aeroplanes* by Jan Mark (Oxford University Press)
*The Wright Brothers (Lives and Times)* by Margaret Hudson (Heinemann Library)
*Flight: 100 Years of Aviation* by R. G. Grant (Dorling Kindersley)

And don't forget....

*Biggles Learns to Fly* by Captain W. E. Johns
(Red Fox)

# Other things to do...

- Find other Greek myths and legends to enjoy – there are plenty of them! Many have a moral, or lesson, for us to learn. Can you identify the moral in each myth? Can you see how the lessons they teach us are still relevant today?

- Conduct further research into the long fascination Man has had with flight. What did the first aeroplanes look like? Were they successful? Put together a short presentation on flight for your class. You should be able to find interesting facts on the Internet and in CD ROMs, encyclopaedias and magazines.

# Chapter 7

## Posting letters

There are no lamps in our village,
And when the owl-and-bat black night
Creeps up low fields
And sidles along the manor walls
5    I walk quickly.

It is winter;
The letters patter from my hand
Into the tin box in the cottage wall;
The gate taps behind me,
10  And the road in the sliver of moonlight
Gleams greasily
Where the tractors have stood.

I have to go under the spread fingers of trees
Under the dark windows of the old man's house,
15  Where the panes in peeling frames
Flash like spectacles
As I tip-toe.
But there is no sound of him in his one room
In the Queen Anne shell,
20  Behind the shutters.

I run past the gates,
Their iron feet gaitered with grass,
Into the church porch,
Perhaps for sanctuary,
25  Standing, hand on the cold door ring,
While above
The tongue-tip of the clock
Clops
Against the hard palate of the tower.

30 The door groans as I push
And
Dare myself to dash
Along the flagstones to the great brass bird,
To put one shrinking hand
35 Upon the gritty lid
Of Black Tom's tomb.

Don't tempt whatever spirits stir
In this damp corner,
But
40 Race down the aisle,
Blunder past font,
Fumble at door,
Leap steps,
Clang iron gate,
45 And patter through the short-cut muddy lane.

Oh, what a pumping of breath
And choking throat
For three letters.
And now there are the cattle
50 Stirring in the straw
So close
I can hear their soft muzzling and coughs;

And there are the bungalows,
And steel-blue miming of the little screen;
55 And the familiar rattle of the latch,
And our own knocker
Clicking like an old friend;
And
I am home.

*(By Gregory Harrison in Stray or Stop — Poetry Themes)*

# Exercise 7.1 ✏️

Answer the following questions using complete sentences.

1. Why is this village particularly dark at night time?

2. What do you think causes the road to 'gleam greasily' (line 11)?

3. (a) What does the poet mean by the phrase 'the spread fingers of trees'?

   (b) What effect does this metaphor have on the reader?

4. In the sixth stanza (verse) the speaker describes how he makes a quick dash through the church. How does the author create a sense of urgency and speed in this stanza? How does it differ from the other stanzas?

5. What is the poet referring to when he writes 'steel-blue miming of the little screen' (line 54)?

· · · · · · · · · · · · · · · · · · · · · · · · · · · · · · · · · · · · · · · · · · · · · · · · ·

# Exercise 7.2 ✏️

Read the letter from *The Rainbow Theatre Company* on the following page and answer questions using complete sentences.

1. We might call this letter a 'sales letter'. What is it actually selling?

2. Is the Rainbow Theatre Company putting on a traditional version of Shakespeare's play?

3. What else will the actors be offering, as well as the hour-long production?

4. In what ways does live theatre help children to read and understand playscripts, according to The Rainbow Theatre Company?

5. Find three words or phrases that the writer has used to make the production sound appealing to readers.

6. Find meanings for the following words. You may use a dictionary. (a) *abridged* (line 14); (b) *benefits* (line 16); (c) *traditional* (line 17); (d) *competitive* (line 24).

## Please note...
The writer of this letter has used punctuation in the addresses (commas and full stops), but many people choose to leave it out nowadays. Either will do; the most important thing is to be consistent.

## Dear Sir...

# The Rainbow Theatre Company

J. A. Smith Esq.,
Headmaster,
St George's School,
Dragon Lane,
5 Knightsville,
ME2 YU1

Rainbow Theatre,
Blue Street,
Greentown,
Indigo,
YRU RED.
Our ref: CG/001
Your ref: JAS
23rd April 2006

Dear Mr Smith,

10 Re: A Tour of Live Shakespeare for Schools

I should like to draw your attention to our exciting new production of Shakespeare's *Midsummer Night's Dream*, which will be touring schools in the region from September to December 2006.

The production is a modern, abridged version of the classic play, lasting approximately one
15 hour, with an opportunity for the audience to question the cast afterwards.

We believe that the experience of seeing live Shakespeare has great benefits for all pupils. Many children struggle at times in trying to understand the meaning of the traditional scripts. At the Rainbow Theatre Company we believe that live performances can bring words to life and create interest and enthusiasm in the audience.

20 Our cast is a small and talented one. We have seven skilled actors and actresses, all of whom have trained at top theatre schools in London and abroad. Our cast has much experience of playing to young audiences and always enjoys the challenge of answering pupils' questions after each show!

Our rates are competitive. For our company to visit your school to perform the play and
25 receive questions, the fee is £275.00. We can come in a morning or afternoon, whichever suits your timetable.

I look forward to hearing from you.

Yours sincerely,

*C. Greasepaint*

# Exercise 7.3 ✏

Your turn to write:

1. Write your own poem about being out at night time. Imagine you are in a place without street lamps and nothing but the moon to light your way. How do you feel? What can you see? Use lots of adjectives, similes and metaphors to describe the scene. Remember to appeal to all five of the reader's senses, as you bring the night to life.

2. Write a story entitled 'The Letter that Changed my Life'. Imagine that the postman delivers an ordinary-looking letter to your door, the contents of which are so exciting that your life is never the same again. Imagine you have won a competition, or have been given a fantastic job. Describe your feelings as you open the letter and show your reaction to reading it.

3. Read the letter from the Rainbow Theatre Company again. Write a reply, in the role of Mr Smith, in which he takes them up on their offer to stage a production at St George's School. Think of some questions that Mr Smith might have for the actors: How much space will they need? Will they require any special facilities, like a sink or a table? Will they need extra parking space? Will they be allowed to record the performance?

4. Write a letter to the headteacher of your school. Your task is to try and sell him or her an exciting new product – a new trampoline for example, or a school piano. Your letter will need to be persuasive and to convince your headteacher that the school simply must have your product. Look again at the letter above and pay close attention to how it is laid out.

. . . . . . . . . . . . . . . . . . . . . . . . . . . . . . . . . . . . . . . . . .

# Learning about language
## Similes and metaphors

*Where the panes in peeling frames*
*Flash like spectacles*

This short quotation from *Posting Letters* contains a **simile** – a phrase that compares two similar things, often using the words 'like' or 'as'. Here, the poet is comparing the windows of the 'old man's house' to a pair of spectacles (linking in well with the old man, who may wear spectacles). Both windows and spectacles have glass in them that flashes when it catches the sunlight.

Other, more well-known, similes include:

*as cold as ice*

*as quiet as a mouse*

*he ran like the wind*

Beware! Some similes, including these examples, have been used so much that they have become **clichés** – expressions that have lost their impact and seem dull because they have been overused. It is always better to invent your own similes.

# Exercise 7.4

The following sentences contain overused similes or clichés. Rewrite each sentence, replacing the phrase underlined with a new, fresher one of your own.

**1.** She had <u>eyes like diamonds</u>.

**2.** David <u>grinned like a cat who'd got the cream</u>.

**3.** The room was <u>as black as night</u>.

**4.** Max charged into the changing room <u>like a bull in a china shop</u>.

**5.** 'I've been <u>as busy as a bee</u>, today,' said Mum.

Look at the following lines, also taken from *Posting Letters*.

*The owl-and-bat black night*

**Creeps** *up low fields*

*And* **sidles** *along the manor walls*

*To put one* **shrinking** *hand*

*Upon the gritty lid*

*Of Black Tom's tomb.*

Can the night *actually* creep or sidle? Is the narrator's hand in the poem *really* shrinking?

These words are used as **metaphors** – words or phrases that should not be taken literally, but are used to create an effect on the reader. Like similes, metaphors compare similar objects, but rather than using 'like' or 'as', they go even further and carry meanings and characteristics across from one word to another. (Hence the word 'metaphor' which comes from a Greek word meaning 'to carry over', or 'transfer'.)

For example:

*Mum was my rock during exams.* (She was a strong and reliable support for me to lean on.)

*We were whipped by the opposition.* (The other team punished us by scoring more goals than we did.)

*The runner's legs were on fire.* (She was running very fast indeed.)

# Exercise 7.5 ✏

Copy the following sentences and next to each one write a 'translation' to show the meaning of the metaphor being used. If these sentences were literally true there would be some pretty peculiar situations!

1. He looked back at the teacher with a blank face.

2. The moon was a precious jewel.

3. By the second half, the team had a mountain to climb.

4. The examinations hung over the children's heads all term.

5. The teacher had eyes in the back of her head.

# Exercise 7.6 ✏

Many metaphors refer to different parts of our body. For example, *She had a long face* (meaning she looked miserable), or *Mum kept her eye on me* (meaning she watched me closely). Can you think of metaphors for each of the following body parts?

1. nose

2. hand

3. face

4. head

5. mouth

## Alliteration

**Alliteration** is a series of words beginning with the same letter or sound. Look at the following examples of alliteration taken from the poem *Posting Letters*.

**gl**eams **gr**easily

**t**ongue-**t**ip of the **cl**ock

**Cl**ops

Repeating letter patterns or sounds in this way has an interesting effect on the words and phrases used – it makes them easier to remember and more appealing to readers. For this reason you will see alliteration not only in stories and poems, but elsewhere in newspaper headlines, shop names and advertising slogans.

For example:

## BRITAIN'S BRAVE BOYS!

Mike's Motors

## Pick up a Penguin!

# Exercise 7.7 🖊

Use alliteration to write catchy headlines, titles and slogans for the following:

1. a hairdressing salon

2. England win the World Cup

3. a new chocolate bar for sale

4. a restaurant

5. the launch of a new luxury ship

. . . . . . . . . . . . . . . . . . . . . . . . . . . . . . . . . . . . . . . . . . . .

# Can you spell?

## Onomatopoeia

Look at the following words, each one taken from the poem *Posting Letters*, and decide what they all have in common.

*patter    clops    clang    rattle    clicking*

The answer, of course, is that they all make the sounds that they describe. In other words, they are spelt in such a way that the letters of the word make the actual sound. This is called **onomatopoeia**. More examples include:

*splash    buzz    tinkle    fizz    pop*

Poets and authors use onomatopoeia frequently to make their writing come alive. When read aloud onomatopoeic phrases are exciting and dramatic. They make the reader feel involved in the story too by hearing the sounds the characters can hear. For example:

*The mud <u>squelched</u> beneath my feet.*

*The drink <u>fizzed</u> in my glass as the bubbles <u>popped</u> at the surface.*

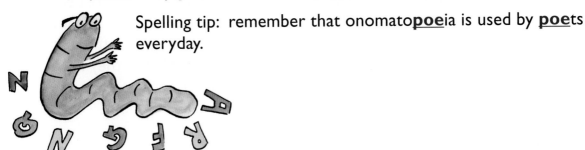

Spelling tip: remember that onomato**poe**ia is used by **poe**ts everyday.

# Exercise 7.8 

Write a sentence of your own for each of the following onomatopoeic words.

1. squeak
2. sizzle
3. snap
4. bang
5. crackle

6. twitter
7. crash
8. hoot
9. howl
10. clang

# Speaking and listening

- Re-read Gregory Harrison's poem, *Posting Letters*. Find a partner and practise reading the poem aloud with each person taking a verse or stanza. See if you can learn your words and then perform the poem aloud. Remember to put lots of expression into your work to appeal to your audience.

- Work with a partner. One of you imagines he or she is the speaker in the poem. The other plays the part of a ghost whom the speaker encounters in the church. Perhaps it is Black Tom up from his tomb! Rehearse a short scene in which the speaker enters the church, places his hand on Black Tom's tomb and receives quite a surprise.

- With a partner act out a telephone conversation between Mr Smith and a representative from The Rainbow Theatre Company in which the headteacher books a team of actors to come and perform at St George's School. What sort of information will the theatre need? What sort of questions will Mr Smith ask?

- In a group of three or four, prepare, rehearse and perform a short sketch in which you play the parts of the actors arriving at St George's School to set up for a production. Mr Smith, the headteacher, greets them at the door. Unfortunately they soon discover one problem – they have forgotten to bring their costumes. How will they cope?

# Have you read?

There are simply hundreds of poetry books for children. Here are some of the best ones.

*The Rattle Bag* edited by Ted Hughes and Seamus Heaney (Faber and Faber)
*Collected Poems for Children* by Ted Hughes, illustrated by Raymond Briggs (Faber and Faber)
*Read Me: A Poem a Day for the National Year of Reading* edited by Gaby Morgan (Macmillan's Children's Books)
*100 Best Poems for Children* edited by Roger McGough (Puffin Books)
*School's Out: Poems not for School* by Benjamin Zephaniah (AK Distribution)
*Collected Poems for Children* by Charles Causley (Macmillan's Children's Books)
*The Oxford Book of Christmas Poems* edited by Michael Harrison and Christopher Stuart-Clark (Oxford University Press)
*The Dragon Book of Verse* edited by Michael Harrison and Christopher Stuart-Clark (Oxford University Press)
*A World of Poetry* edited by Michael Rosen (Kingfisher Books)
*Posting Letters: Poems* by Gregory Harrison (Oxford University Press)

· · · · · · · · · · · · · · · · · · · · · · · · · · · · · · · · · · · · · · · · · · · · · · ·

# Other things to do...

- Find out more about the history of posting letters. Today we simply place a stamp on the envelope and, as if by magic, the letter arrives the next morning. But was it always like that? How was our mail delivered many years ago? Was it reliable? Use the Internet, CD ROMs, books and magazines to find out more. You could begin by researching the history of The Royal Mail.

- Find real sales letters that are advertising a new product of some kind. You will probably have plenty at home (sometimes we call it 'junk mail'). Look at the language that is used to persuade readers to pick up the telephone and buy the product. Will you fall for the sales talk? Be careful not to spend your parents' money!

# Chapter 8

## Behind the wheel

Blinded by his love of motor cars, Toad ends up in court charged with reckless driving – but can he persuade the magistrate to let him off?

**Magistrate**   I understand that the prisoner is a member of the middle classes and has a charming home in a riverside setting, parts of which date back to the fourteenth century.  Moreover he regularly sits down to meals of at least five courses, besides which, and one might think that this is the
5   clincher, he doesn't have to do his own washing-up.  Is that right?

**Toad**   Quite right.  I've never done the washing-up in my life.

**Magistrate**   I'm glad to hear it. That is one side of the picture… The other need not detain us long. The prisoner has been accused of taking and driving away a motor car, apropos of which I'd just like to ask the court
10   one question. Why should the prisoner, a person of means, steal a motor car when he can, as we have heard, just as easily buy one?

**Chief Weasel**   Why should he buy one when he can just as easily steal one?

**Magistrate**   I hadn't thought of that. Are you a witness?

**Chief Weasel**   No, your honour.  Just a weasel with the public interest at
15   heart.

**Magistrate**  Now the prisoner is alleged to have driven the car into a pond. Tell me, have you ever driven into a pond before?

**Toad**   No, your honour.

**Magistrate**   So this is a first offence?

20   **Ferret Fred**   He's driven into a haystack.

**Magistrate**   Really?  Who are you?  Identify yourself.

**Ferret Fred**   I'm just a ferret who cares for justice, your honour.

**Magistrate**  Well, a haystack and a pond are a very different kettle of fish so I'm going to ignore that.

25   **Stoat Stuart**   He had a close shave with a cow, your honour.

**Magistrate** Dear, oh dear! And who are you?

**Stoat Stuart** A stoat who knows the difference between right and wrong, your honour.

**Magistrate** I don't like the sound of a close shave with a cow.

30 **Clerk** Is the cow in court, your honour?

**Magistrate** I don't know. Is the cow in court?

**Chief Weasel** Yes, your honour.

*There is an awkward pause until the Chief Weasel nudges Weasel Norman, and though he is hardly a cow look-alike he dutifully stands up.*

35 **Rat** That's not a cow, your honour. It's a weasel.

**Weasel Norman** I'm a cow.

**Rat** You are a weasel.

**Weasel Norman** I'm a cow. Moo.

*There is pandemonium in the court, shouts of 'Cow!' 'Cow!' and counter-cries of*
40 *'Weasel!' 'Weasel!'*

**Magistrate** Stop it, stop it. Whether the witness is a cow or a weasel might exercise an Oxford philosopher but it need not detain us here.

**Fox** Sir, sir.

**Magistrate** Oh, I'm fed up with being interrupted. What is it?

45 **Fox** The prisoner's driving brought a hen of my acquaintance to the brink of nervous collapse. She didn't know whether she was coming or going.

**Magistrate** Hens never do know whether they're coming or going.

**Fox** This one did. She was very single-minded. Only now she's lost her head completely.

50 **Magistrate** And who are you?

**Fox** I'm a fox with a conscience.

**Badger** Ha!

**Magistrate**   I don't want to hear any more. Despite all these objections I still retain the favourable impression I had of the prisoner when he first
55 stepped into the dock. I keep thinking of that riverside mansion, where who knows I might one day be a guest…

*Toad has begun to doze off and it takes a poke from Rat to alert him to the benefits that might accrue from an offer of hospitality.*

**Toad**   Oh yes. Any time you please. It will be a pleasure.

60 **Magistrate**   Oh that's very kind of you…though that does not affect my judgement in the least. Do you do kedgeree for breakfast at all?

**Toad**   Oh yes. And devilled kidneys.

**Magistrate**   Oh my
65 favourite. However kedgeree and kidneys to one side, my inclination is to let the prisoner go free. With
70 one small proviso, namely the prisoner must never under any circumstances go near a motor car again. He
75 must never ever drive.

**Clerk**   What do you say to that?

**Toad**   *(very subdued)* Never.

**Magistrate**   Excellent. Case dismissed.

**Toad**   No. Stop. I don't mean I never will. I mean I never won't.

80 **Magistrate**   You never won't what?

**Toad**   I never won't…not drive. I love motor cars. Motoring is my destiny! Petrol runs in my blood. I was born to drive. Poop poop. Poop poop.

*(From The Wind in the Willows by Kenneth Grahame, adapted for the stage by Alan Bennett)*

# Exercise 8.1 🖉

Read the extract from *The Wind in the Willows* and answer the following questions using complete sentences.

1.  What is the crime that Toad has been accused of?

2.  What do you think is meant by the phrase 'a person of means' (line 10)?

3.  Is the cow actually in court (line 30)? Explain your answer by referring closely to the passage.

4.  Bribery is when you persuade someone to make a particular decision by giving him money, gifts or favours. Do you think this judge is open to bribery? Try to support your answer with evidence from the passage.

5.  Does Toad accept his punishment without question?

6.  Find, and then write down, a definition for each of the following words:
    (a) *clincher* (line 5); (b) *alleged* (line 16); (c) *justice* (line 22); (d) *conscience* (line 51).

## The drive of your life

Sales brochures are well-known for their persuasive language. Their purpose is, after all, to persuade readers to buy the product they are selling. Here, the Morgan Motor Company invites us to consider its new 'Roadster'.

The classic Morgan returns, retaining all of its traditional qualities and timeless appearance but with a reinvigorated heart: a new power unit, making it lighter, more agile, faster.

5   This is a sports car unlike any other. Unequivocally a driver's car, a true original, that is, without doubt, emotionally sensational. The stunning new Morgan Roadster – now, for a limited period, available in North America.

The worthy successor...

How do you follow the legendary Plus 8?

With the new Morgan Roadster, that's how!

10   Powerful, smooth and flexible, this new 225 bhp 3 litre lightweight

redefines the Morgan driving experience.

A 'once only' production run of just 82 cars guarantees exclusivity – the unique Morgan fusion of traditional coach building techniques, only the best materials and modern engine technology, guarantees a pleasure of
15 ownership simply unavailable anywhere else.

Balance and poise...

Drive a Morgan Roadster and truly appreciate what it's like to be in control of a modern sports car. With a low centre of gravity and near perfect weight distribution the new Roadster has outstanding balance
20 and poise. Peer down the long bonnet, accelerate, and indulge your senses. Hear the new V6 power unit howl into life, feel the rush of the landscape whilst the new Roadster involves you in an unparalleled driving experience.

Latest engine technology...

25 How do you improve upon an icon? With the latest lightweight 3 litre V6 engine technology.

Meeting all the latest world standards in engine emissions and fuel economy, the new power unit propels traditional Morgan motoring into a new era. Drive the dream. Drive a Morgan Roadster.

# Exercise 8.2 ✏

Read the extract entitled *The drive of your life* and answer the following questions using complete sentences.

1. What is the new feature that allows the car to feel lighter and more agile?

2. Which car came before the new Morgan Roadster?

3. What do you think is meant by the phrase 'redefines the Morgan driving experience' (line 11)?

4. How is the car able to have such outstanding balance?

5. (a) Whom do you think this writing is aimed at?

   (b) What is its purpose?

6. This text is packed with powerful, persuasive adjectives. Find two examples of these and describe the effects they may have on the reader.

7. Find dictionary definitions for the following words: (a) *reinvigorated* (line 2); (b) *sensational* (line 5); (c) *successor* (line 7); (d) *exclusivity* (line 12).

. . . . . . . . . . . . . . . . . . . . . . . . . . . . . . . . . . . . . . . . . . . .

# Exercise 8.3 ✏

Your turn to write:

1. Look again at the extract from *The Wind in the Willows*. Imagine you are a newspaper journalist sent to the courtroom to prepare a report on Toad's trial. Write a description of what happens in court. You will need to think about the crime, the judge's comments, Toad's behaviour, the final judgement and the constant interruptions by the witnesses.

2. Imagine you are the owner of the car that Toad stands accused of taking. You saw him take it and then reported the theft to the police. You are now in the witness box, describing what you saw and whom you think is responsible for stealing your car. Write a short scene in which you have to answer questions about what you saw and when.

3.  Re-read the passage entitled *The drive of your life*. Choose a different car – it may be a real car that you know a lot about, or an imaginary one – and then write a similar piece of persuasive writing in which you describe its remarkable features. Remember to use interesting adjectives that will grab readers' attention and persuade them to go out and buy this make of car.

4.  Write a story about a car that has special powers like Chitty Chitty Bang Bang. Perhaps your car can fly or dive underwater. Who will drive the car? Where will he or she take it? Will other people want to get their hands on your magic car? Make your story as thrilling as possible by including lots of exciting action and plenty of imaginative description.

# Learning about language

## Idioms

Idioms are phrases or other groups of words which have a meaning other than their logical one. The following phrases, taken from the extract from *The Wind in the Willows*, are all idioms:

'*a very different kettle of fish*' (line 23)

'*a close shave*' (line 25)

'*petrol runs in my blood*' (line 82)

An idiom is a phrase that may seem peculiar when taken literally, but one that has a special meaning of its own. This meaning may have nothing to do with the real meanings of the individual words within it. 'Hard cheese' for example, is not referring to cheese that has gone hard: as an idiom it means 'bad luck'.

Idioms are different from metaphors. An idiom usually means something completely different – cheese has nothing to do with luck and petrol has nothing to do with blood.

A metaphor, on the other hand, is making comparisons and suggesting ways in which the thing being described is similar to something else. 'The spread fingers of the trees' in 'Posting Letters' (Chapter 7) is a metaphor likening the branches of the trees to human fingers.

Consequently idioms cannot be translated properly into other languages, because their special meanings are normally peculiar to one language only.

The 'kettle of fish' for example, that the magistrate refers to in the extract means an awkward situation or predicament and one that is difficult to get out of.

To have a 'close shave' means narrowly to avoid a disaster or accident. (Presumably Toad nearly hit a cow in his motor car.)

Finally, to say something 'runs in your blood' means you inherited an interest or passion for it – you 'were born to do it'. In the play, Toad says he was 'born to drive' and this is what he also means when he says petrol runs in his blood (because petrol is fuel for cars).

· · · · · · · · · · · · · · · · · · · · · · · · · · · · · · · · · · · · · · · · · · ·

# Exercise 8.4

Copy the following idioms and next to each one write its accepted meaning. The first one has been done for you.

1. a piece of cake – *easy to do, requiring little or no effort*

2. on thin ice

3. barking up the wrong tree

4. heads will roll!

5. to turn over a new leaf

6. to see eye to eye

7. to lose face

8. to keep an eye on something

9. the lion's share

10. to have other fish to fry

# Exercise 8.5

Each of the following sentences contains an idiom. Explain in your own words what each sentence actually means. The first has been done for you.

1. David knew he would have to eat humble pie when he got home.

   *David knew that he was going to have to apologise humbly when he got home.*

2. The investigators soon managed to get to the heart of the problem.

3. The children made a bee-line for the sweet shop.

4. After suffering a cold, Michelle was left with a frog in her throat.

5. Mr Simmons was forced to sell the house lock, stock and barrel.

6. The plan was going well until Michael threw a spanner in the works.

7. On the day of the results the students were on tenterhooks.

8. When Jane returned from Guide camp, she slept like a log.

9. 'I like to call a spade a spade,' said Grandad.

10. After months of arguing, the pair agreed to bury the hatchet.

## Imperative forms of verbs

Sometimes known as commands or orders, imperative forms of verbs give instructions to readers or listeners. They tell people what to do, think or say – but they can be used gently to persuade readers too. Imperatives are often used in recipes, directions, instructions and various persuasive texts like brochures for cars and holidays.

Look at the following examples, taken from *The drive of your life*.

'**Drive** *a Morgan Roadster…*'

'**Peer** *down the long bonnet…*'

'**Hear** *the new V6 power unit…*'

In these examples, the verbs to drive, to peer and to hear are used in the imperative form to invite, or persuade, readers to go out and test drive a Morgan Roadster.  See how the following alternatives seem less persuasive:

If you drive a Morgan Roadster you will appreciate….

If you peer down the long bonnet….

If you listen to the new V6 power unit….

Imperatives are more direct. They are useful tools in attracting the attention of your readers and 'reeling them in' (another idiom!).

# Exercise 8.6 ✏

Copy the following sentences and underline the imperative(s) in each.

1.  Relax beneath the shade of a palm tree.

2.  Feel the silky smooth sand between your toes and hear the waves lapping against the shore.

3.  Switch into fifth gear, accelerate and enjoy the ride of your life.

4.  Sunshine holidays: let your worries drift away.

5.  Call your local showroom for details.

# Can you spell?

## Synonyms
Synonyms are different words with similar meanings, for example: big, large, enormous, gigantic, colossal, huge.

Synonyms are very useful when we want to make our writing as interesting as possible.  By using different synonyms we can avoid repeating ourselves and, if we make the effort to search for the more interesting synonyms each time, our writing will never become bland or boring.

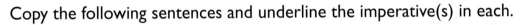

For example, in the passage *The drive of your life*, rather than saying 'emotionally sensational' (line 5), the writers could have said 'good fun' or 'nice to drive'. Or, instead of saying the 'stunning' new Morgan Roadster they could have described the car as 'lovely' or 'great'. Which do you think is more exciting? Which will attract readers' attention and make them want to go out and buy a Morgan?

## Exercise 8.7

Can you think of synonyms for the following words? Copy each one and then write a more interesting synonym next to it.

1. small

2. happy

3. sad

4. scared

5. old

## Exercise 8.8

The best place to find synonyms is in a **thesaurus** – either in a book or on a computer. Here you will find words listed alphabetically, as in a dictionary, but rather than definitions you will see a list of synonyms.

Find the following words in a thesaurus and then write down three more interesting synonyms next to each one.

1. fast

2. nice

3. loud

4. lazy

5. charming

# Exercise 8.9 ✏

The following sentences and phrases are all taken from *The Wind in the Willows*. Copy each one and replace the word in blue with a more interesting synonym of your own. Line references have been included to enable you to revisit the quotations and choose the synonym that best fits the sentences as they appear in the passage.

1.  Is that **right?** (line 5)

2.  I'm **glad** to hear it. (line 7)

3.  The prisoner has been accused of **taking** and driving away a motor car. (lines 8–9)

4.  Oh that's very **kind** of you… (line 60)

5.  With one small **proviso**… (line 69-70)

. . . . . . . . . . . . . . . . . . . . . . . . . . . . . . . . . . . . . . . . . . . . .

# Speaking and listening

1.  Put on a performance of the passage from *The Wind in the Willows*, each person taking on the rôle of a character from the play. You may perform it as a whole class, or in groups. Try to learn your own lines by heart so that you can think about other features of your production such as stage positions, movement and expression.

2.  Hot-seating: Take turns to be one of the characters from the play. Sit in the 'hot seat' at the front of the classroom and answer questions from your friends about how you felt in court – and what you think of Mister Toad.

3.  Class debate: Write a short speech agreeing, or disagreeing, with the following motion: *This house believes that motor cars are too dangerous. We should ban them from all town centres so that we may shop in peace and safety.* Once you have written your speech, join in a class debate in which you can present your viewpoint. Listen carefully to your friends' opinions too.

# Have you read?

The following stories and non-fiction books all involve cars of one sort or another.

*Cars* by Paul May (Oxford University Press)
*Ice Mountain* by Darrice Bailer (et al.) (Little Simon)
*What Makes a Car Go?* Sophy Tahta (Usborne Publishing)
*Mrs Armitage: Queen of the Road* by Quentin Blake (Illustrator)
(Peachtree Publishers)
*I-Spy Classic Cars* (I-Spy)
*Cars (Past and Present)* by Neil Morris (Belitha Press)
*All About Cars* by Peter Harrison (Southwater)
*Everything I Know about Cars* by Tom Lichtenheld
(Simon and Schuster Children's Publishing)
*To the Rescue* by Cecile Schoberla (Little Simon)
*Cars, Trains and Motorbikes (How Science Works)*
by Chris Oxlade (Franklin Watts)

# Other things to do...

- Find a copy of Alan Bennett's complete play version of *The Wind in the Willows*, originally a novel by Kenneth Grahame, and read it with your friends. You may even be able to persuade your teacher to stage it as your next school production.

- Collect brochures for cars, boats or houses. As you read them make a note of the persuasive adjectives and the imperatives they use to persuade readers to buy their product. Once you have read a few examples, design your own sales brochure for an exciting new type of aeroplane or space rocket.

# Chapter 9

## The earwig nest

From a very early age, author and naturalist Gerald Durrell always had a fascination for creatures of all kinds – even earwigs...

Perhaps the most exciting discovery I made in this multi-coloured Lilliput to which I had access was an earwig's nest. I had long wanted to find one and had searched everywhere without success, so the joy of stumbling upon one unexpectedly was overwhelming, like suddenly being given a
5   wonderful present. I moved a piece of bark and there beneath it was the nursery, a small hollow in the earth that the insect must have burrowed out for herself. She squatted in the middle of it, shielding underneath her a few white eggs. She crouched over them like a hen, and did not move when the flood sunlight struck her as I lifted the bark. I could not count
10   the eggs, but there did not seem to be many, so I presumed that she had not yet laid her full complement. Tenderly I replaced her lid of bark.

From that moment I guarded the nest jealously. I erected a protecting wall of rocks round it, and as an additional precaution I wrote out a notice in red ink and stuck it on a pole nearby as a warning to the family. The
15   notice read: 'BEWAR – EARWIG NEST – * QUIAT PLESE.' It was only remarkable in that the two correctly spelt words were biological ones. Every hour or so I would subject the mother earwig to ten minutes' close scrutiny. I did not dare examine her more often for fear she might desert her nest. Eventually the pile of eggs beneath her grew, and she seemed to
20   have become accustomed to my lifting off her bark roof. I even decided that she began to recognize me, from the friendly way she waggled her antennae.

To my acute disappointment, after all my efforts and constant sentry duty,
25   the babies hatched out during the night. I felt that, after all I had done, the female might have held up the hatching until I was there to witness it. However, there they
30   were, a fine brood of young earwigs, minute, frail, looking as

though they had been carved out of ivory. They moved gently under their mother's body, walking between her legs, the more venturesome even climbing on to her pincers. It was a heart-warming sight. The next day the nursery was empty: my wonderful family had scattered over the garden. I
35  saw one of the babies some time later: he was bigger, of course, browner and stronger, but I recognized him immediately. He was curled up in a maze of rose-petals, having a sleep, and when I disturbed him he merely raised his pincers irritably over his back. I would have liked to think that it was a salute, a cheerful greeting, but honesty compelled me to admit that
40  it was nothing more than an earwig's warning to a potential enemy. Still, I excused him. After all, he had been very young when I last saw him.

*(From My Family and Other Animals by Gerald Durrell)*

# Exercise 9.1 🖉

Read the extract from *My Family and Other Animals* and answer these questions using full sentences.

1. Why was it especially overwhelming for Gerald to stumble upon an earwig's nest?

2. (a) What happened to the insect as Gerald lifted the bark?

   (b) How did the insect react to this change?

3. There is evidence in the passage to suggest that Gerald struggled with spelling as a child, and yet he was able to spell the names of animals and plants perfectly. What does this tell you about him?

4. What made Gerald think that the earwig might actually recognise him?

5. How did the baby earwig react when Gerald disturbed him?

6. Find two words or phrases in the passage that reveal Gerald's enthusiasm and interest for insects of this kind.

7. Use a dictionary to help you write definitions for the following words:
   (a) *complement* (line 11); (b) *tenderly* (line 11); (c) *scrutiny* (line 18);
   (d) *brood* (line 30).

## Earwigs

You may have heard that earwigs will crawl into your ear while you are lying down or asleep but this is not true. People may have thought this because earwigs hide in dark, narrow and cool places such as under the bark of a tree or stones. They may have got their name because some of them have wings shaped like ears – and the name 'earwings' was changed to 'earwigs'.

Earwigs have a narrow, dark brown body with pincers at the rear end which they use to defend themselves and use in courtship displays. The pincers are rounded in the male and straighter in the female so it is easy to tell the girls from the boys. Not all species of earwigs have wings but even those with wings rarely use them, perhaps because they have to fold them very carefully and tightly under their wing cases. Earwigs are usually nocturnal and come out to feed at night, eating aphids, small caterpillars and plants.

In the autumn the female earwig will lay about 40 tiny eggs which she carefully hides in a burrow which she has dug, sometimes under a stone or piece of wood. Unlike many other insects she will look after them until they hatch in the spring, and she will continue to protect them until they are about two weeks old. She guards the eggs with great care and will gather them together if they are moved by other insects or foraging birds, and will clean them in her mouth if they get dirty.

When the nymphs hatch in spring they are pale and almost see-through, gradually becoming darker as they grow which they do by shedding their skin and growing a new one. They will moult their skin about five times until they reach their adult size.

# Exercise 9.2 ✏️

Read the above passage and answer these questions using full sentences.

1. Name two places where an earwig likes to hide.

2. How might earwigs have earned their unusual name?

3. How do earwigs use their pincers?

4. How can you tell the difference between male and female earwigs?

5. What evidence is there to suggest that female earwigs make good mothers?

6. Describe the ways in which newborn earwigs change as they grow older.

7. Use a dictionary to help you write definitions for the following words:
   (a) *pincers* (line 7); (b) *species* (line 11); (c) *nocturnal* (line 13); (d) *moult* (line 29).

# Exercise 9.3 ✏️

Your turn to write:

1. Have you ever lifted an old piece of bark, or a stone in the garden, to see what is underneath? Imagine you do just that and find a family of tiny insects lurking beneath. Choose a different group of insect from earwigs: perhaps woodlice, ants or beetles. Remember to give the reader a detailed description, including a guess at what the insects are thinking and feeling.

2. Imagine you are the mother earwig in the extract from *My Family and Other Animals*. What must it feel like to have your ceiling of bark suddenly raised, to be flooded with blinding sunlight and then have a pair of giant eyes staring down at you? Write a short piece of writing in which you describe the experience from the earwig's point of view.

3. Use the information available in the passage about earwigs to design and produce a poster 'all about earwigs'. You will need to include:

   - a paragraph of introduction
   - a diagram or sketch of an earwig
   - annotations (labels)
   - captions
   - paragraphs with sub-headings

# Learning about language

## Apostrophes

Apostrophes (') serve two main purposes in writing:

- They show when one or more letters have been left out (we call this 'omission' or 'contraction').

- They indicate when something belongs to someone (we call this 'possession').

## Apostrophes to show omission / contraction

Sometimes – particularly when we are talking – we shorten words and phrases to make them quicker, or easier, to say.

We might say, for example, 'I've' instead of 'I have', or 'he'll' instead of 'he will'.

We omit (leave out) some letters, so the words become shorter – or 'contracted'.

Look at the following lines taken from the information text on Earwigs.

'they **don't** really crawl into people's ears'

'but **it's** quite rare for them to fly'

Which letters do you think the writer has omitted here? What would be the full versions of the words in blue?

. . . . . . . . . . . . . . . . . . . . . . . . . . . . . . . . . . . . . . . . . . .

# Exercise 9.4

In the following sentences apostrophes have been used in place of certain letters to make contractions. Rewrite each sentence replacing the contracted words with their full versions.

1. Look! I've found a nest of earwigs.

2. If I were an earwig I wouldn't like my nest being disturbed.

3. Won't you come with me? You'll enjoy seeing the nest.

4. I'd rather be an ant than an earwig.

5. Earwigs like to eat plants but they'll eat other insects too, if they get the chance.

Beware of **it's** and **its**. The first is a contraction like the ones above, where the apostrophe shows us that the letter 'i' or 'ha' has been left out (the full version is 'it is' or 'it has').

The second is not a contraction at all. It is a possessive pronoun (i.e. The dog ate its bone) and, like *his*, *her* or *my*, it does not need an apostrophe.

## Exercise 9.5

Write out the following words and next to each write a contracted version. The first one is done for you.

**1.** you will – *you'll*

**2.** I have

**3.** will not

**4.** can not

**5.** do not

**6.** we are

Contractions like these are considered informal, or 'chatty'. We usually just reserve them for when we quote what people have actually said or for fictional dialogue in stories. You can use contractions if you wish – but make sure you don't (or do not!) use them in formal comprehension answers.

## Apostrophes to show possession

Look at the following phrases, taken from the first passage:

'an earwig's nest'

'under their mother's body'

In the first example, the apostrophe tells us that the nest belongs to the earwig.

In the second example, it tells us that the body belongs to their mother.

Here are some more general examples of apostrophes being used to show possession:

the dog's bone – the bone belonging to the dog

Michael's tennis racket – the racket belonging to Michael

the team's trophies – the trophies won by the team

· · · · · · · · · · · · · · · · · · · · · · · · · · · · · · · · · · · · · · · · · · · · · · · · · · · · · ·

# Exercise 9.6 ✏

Copy out each of the following phrases and next to each one write a shorter version using an apostrophe to show possession. The first has been done for you.

1.  The car belonging to the teacher – *the teacher's car*

2.  The whiskers belonging to the cat –

3.  The truncheon belonging to the policeman –

4.  The bag belonging to the postman –

5.  The nest belonging to the bird –

So, when we wish to show that something belongs to someone, we put an apostrophe after their name and then add an '–s'.

But what happens when the word already ends in '–s', like James, or Ross? The answer is, we usually add an apostrophe and another '–s' to make:

St James's Church

Ross's mother

However, the normal convention in the case of Jesus is not to add an 's' after the apostrophe, e.g. in Jesus' name.

Some plurals end in '–s' too, like *animals* or *cars*, and in these cases we add an apostrophe but NOT another '–s'. So we get:

The boys' coats

The girls' pencil cases

The dogs' kennel

# Exercise 9.7

Rewrite these phrases using an apostrophe. Some words are plurals and others are not. The first has been done for you.

1. The bag of Charles – *Charles's bag*

2. The mother of Miss Atkins

3. The pencil of Lucas

4. The food of the penguins

5. The church of St Thomas

6. The locker room of the players

· · · · · · · · · · · · · · · · · · · · · · · · · · · · · · · · · · · · · ·

# Can you spell?

## Antonyms

A synonym is a word meaning the same as another word. An **antonym** is a word that means the opposite of another word. For example:

good  –  bad

high  –  low

Antonyms are sometimes formed by adding a prefix to another word:

possible  –  **im**possible

usual  –  **un**usual

Suffixes are also useful for switching between antonyms:

harm**ful**  –  harm**less**

worthy  –  worth**less**

Beware! Some words may look like antonyms of other words but they are not. For example, if something is *priceless* it does not mean it is free – it means it is so valuable that it is beyond price.

Similarly, *valuable* and *invaluable* look like antonyms but they are not: *invaluable* actually means very valuable indeed – beyond any ordinary value.

# Exercise 9.8 🖉

Copy out the following words and write an appropriate antonym next to each one. The first one has been done for you. A good dictionary or thesaurus may help you.

1. early – *late*
2. ungrateful
3. happy
4. unlucky
5. hopeless

6. legal
7. incomplete
8. merciful
9. convenient
10. honest

. . . . . . . . . . . . . . . . . . . . . . . . . . . . . . . . . . . . . . . . . . . . . .

# Exercise 9.9 🖉

Write sentences for each pair of antonyms to show that you understand the differences in meaning. Again the first pair has been completed for you as an example.

1. high – *The river was high and there was a risk of flooding.*

   low – *Peter was disappointed with his low grades.*

2. friendly –

   unfriendly –

3. open –

   closed –

4. useful –

   useless –

5. behave –

   misbehave –

# Speaking and listening

1. Hot-seating: Find a partner to work with. Take turns in pretending to be Gerald Durrell. Invite your partner to ask you questions about the time you discovered the earwig nest beneath the piece of wood. Then invite general questions about why you are so fascinated by creatures.

2. TV presenters: Working with one or two friends, imagine you are presenting a children's wildlife programme. This week, the theme is 'miniature worlds' and you will begin by looking at earwigs. Explain in detail for the viewers at home what earwigs are like, where they are found, what they eat, and so on. Present your piece to the class when you are ready.

3. Mastermind: Find a partner to work with. Each write a set of questions on earwigs. Then put your own questions to the other person on 'the life of an earwig'. You will need to revise from the above passages first. Once you have done that, choose other insects to research and then answer questions on.

# Have you read?

The following books by or about Gerald Durrell recount his many travels across the world, studying and appreciating animals of all kinds.

*A Zoo in my Luggage* by Gerald Durrell (Penguin)
*Overloaded Ark* by Gerald Durrell (Faber and Faber)
*Menagerie Manor* by Gerald Durrell (House of Stratus)
*Golden Bats and Pink Pigeons* by Gerald Durrell (House of Stratus)
*The Best of Durrell* Foreward Princess Anne & Introduction Lee Durrell (HarperCollins)
*Birds, Beasts and Relatives* by Gerald Durrell (House of Stratus)
*Encounters with Animals* by Gerald Durrell (Starhaven)

Or try reading these interesting non-fictional books on insects and become an expert like Gerald Durrell.

*Life in the Undergrowth* by David Attenborough (BBC Books)
*Ladybirds and Beetles (Looking at Minibeasts)* by Sally Morgan (Belitha Press Ltd.)
*I Wonder Why Spiders Spin Webs and Other Questions about Creepy-crawlies (I Wonder Why Series)* by Amanda O'Neill (Kingfisher)
*Minibeasts: The World of Invertebrates and Insects (Creative Science Activity Packs)* by G. Alan Revill (David Fulton Publishers)
*Stick Insects (Keeping Unusual Pets Series)* by June McNicholas (Heinemann Library)

# Other things to do...

- Find out more about the weird and wonderful world of insects. You can find lots of interesting information on these websites: www.bbc.co.uk/nature and www.cfz.org.uk. Did you know that there is a National Insect Week held every year? To find out more, visit the following site: www.nationalinsectweek.co.uk

- Choose another insect – something interesting, like a stick insect or a praying mantis. See what you can find out about your insect from books, magazines and Internet sites. Then make a project book all about it. You might want to think about:

  - where it comes from

  - how large it is

  - what it eats

  - how long it may live for

  - names for the different parts of its body

- Write a story of your own in which the main character discovers a giant nest of insects in a very unusual place – perhaps under a pillow, inside a shoe, or in a school bag. Describe the character's reaction to finding it, and remember to explain what happens to the nest in the end.

# Chapter 10

## Down the Amazon

The journey down the Amazon was one that Maia never forgot.  In places the river was so wide that she understood why it was called the River Sea and they sailed between distant lines of trees.  But sometimes they made their way between islands and then, on the sandbanks, they saw some
5  of the creatures that Maia had read about.  Once a litter of capybaras lumbered after their mother and they were close enough to see their funny snouts and sandy fur.  Once they passed a tree whose roots had been killed by the rise of the water, and its bare branches were full of scarlet and blue parakeets which flew up, screeching, when the boat came
10  past. And once Maia saw a grey log lying in the shallows which suddenly came to life.

'Oh look,' she said, 'A croc – I mean an alligator.  My first one!' and a man standing close by nodded, and said he was glad that she knew there were no crocodiles in this part of the world.  'You'd be surprised how many
15  people never learn.'

They passed plantations of rubber trees and Indian villages with the houses built on stilts to stop them being flooded when the river rose. The Indian children came out onto the landing stage and waved and called out, and Maia waved back and didn't stop till they were out of sight.

20  Sometimes the boat went close enough to the shore for them to pass by old houses owned by the sugar planters or coffee exporters; they could see the verandas with the families taking tea, and dogs stretched out in the shade, and hanging baskets of scarlet flowers.

*(From Journey to the River Sea by Eva Ibbotson)*

# Exercise 10.1

Answer these questions using full sentences.

1.  Why do you think the river is referred to as the River Sea?

2.  Why do you think Maia thought the alligator was a log?

3.  Why were the houses built on stilts?

4.  List all the animals mentioned in the passage.

5.  Do you think the Indian children were pleased to see Maia? Support your answer with evidence from the passage.

6.  List the different colours mentioned in the passage.

7.  Write short definitions for the following words. You may use a dictionary. (a) *litter* (line 5); (b) *lumbered* (line 6); (c) *verandas* (line 22).

8.  Do you think Maia enjoyed her trip along the River Sea? Try to support your answer by referring to words and phrases in the passage.

## Dawn on board

*Sunday 28th March.* It is five a.m. I rise to the start of the ship's main engine. Feel grotty and puffy: right side of face looks like a boxer's, a swelling on the cheekbone, due to overexposure to a really burning sun when I was sitting reading on the deck yesterday. I put my T-shirt on and

5   go down to the prow.  Under my bare feet the iron deck is greasy with oil
    and the remains of smoked fish.  It is cool, the river is dead flat, like glass
    or mother-of-pearl.  Not the slightest shimmer on the surface. The sky
    is perfectly reflected in the water: a pale wash with a beautiful white and
    purple cloud formation upriver, faint bands of ultramarine and pink; to the
10  north, over the forest, a cloudless sky with a single puff of purple. Where
    the sky meets the river in the distance a few low-flying islands float in
    a liquid haze. And there is the faintest breeze!  Sometimes on the river,
    as now, or at sunset, the air blows so lightly, so gently, so voluptuously
    soft, that you imagine you could be breathing in deliciousness itself. This
15  enchantment lasts only a moment. The sun appears ahead, just above the
    horizon, just behind a thin band of cloud.  It is a clearly distinct, pale-red
    ball. As it moves higher, and you can watch it rise every second, it emerges
    from each belt of cloud brighter and whiter until it bursts out white-hot
    with a scorching halo illuminating our track upriver like moonlight. A
20  wind comes up and ripples the whole river surface. Then the heat of the
    day begins.

*(From The Congo by Michael Wood in River Journeys by the BBC, London)*

# Exercise 10.2 🖊

Answer these questions using full sentences.

1. Why is Michael's cheekbone swollen?

2. Michael describes the river as 'dead flat, like glass or mother-of pearl'. Write an alternative simile to describe the appearance of the river.

3. Describe the effect that the faint breeze has on Michael.

4. Why does the 'enchantment' last for only a moment? What causes the cool air to change?

5. Describe how the writer's mood changes as the new day begins.

6. List all the different colours mentioned in the passage.

7. Copy the following words and next to each say if it is a verb, noun, adjective or adverb. To help you decide, look at each word and the sentence that surrounds it in the passage: (a) *rise* (line 1); (b) *yesterday* (line 4); (c) *greasy* (line 5); (d) *deliciousness* (line 14).

# Exercise 10.3 🖊

Your turn to write:

1. Have you ever been on a journey that left a lasting impression on you? Have you sailed, trekked, flown or climbed somewhere special? Write a short travel log, like Michael Wood's, that describes a particular stretch of journey. Remember to include your reactions to what you can see, hear and feel.

2. Re-read the passage entitled *Down the Amazon*. Then write a story of your own in which one or more characters enjoy an adventure along the River Amazon. Use adjectives, similes and metaphors to describe the sights and sounds of the river and don't forget to mention the alligators disguised as floating logs.

3.  Imagine you are working for a holiday company specialising in action-packed trips down the Amazon. Your task is to write a feature to appear in the new season's holiday brochure designed to persuade holidaymakers to book a trip with you. You will need to describe the memorable adventures they can experience and the facilities you can offer to make their Amazon safari a trip to remember.

4.  Imagine you are Michael Wood, the author of 'The Congo' in *River Journeys*. You decide to write a letter, or postcard, to your family in which you describe the highs and lows of navigating the world's second greatest river, the Congo.

5.  Write a descriptive poem about a river journey. Select words and phrases for their sound as well as their meaning. Whisk the reader away to a distant land, where he or she can breathe in the 'deliciousness' of an early morning breeze and see tropical skies reflected in seas of glass.

. . . . . . . . . . . . . . . . . . . . . . . . . . . . . . . . . . . . . . . . . . . .

# Learning about language

Look again at the two passages above. They have a lot in common. Both are about a river journey. Both use adjectives, similes and metaphors to describe the sights and sounds of a river. Both have one central character. However, there are also two major differences between the two passages:

*   one is written in the **first** person, while the other uses the **third** person;

*   one uses the **past** tense, while the other is written in the **present** tense.

## First and third person
Read the following sentences, the first of which is from *Down the Amazon*.

*In places the river was so wide that* **she** *understood why it was called the River Sea and* **they** *sailed between distant lines of trees.*

*In places the river was so wide that* **I** *understood why it was called the River Sea and* **we** *sailed between distant lines of trees.*

In the first sentence, the pronoun 'she' refers to Maia. 'They' refers to Maia and the other people with whom she shares the boat. These are **third person pronouns**.

In the second sentence, Maia has been replaced with the pronoun 'I' and the whole group becomes 'we'. These are called **first person pronouns**.

Here are the personal pronouns laid out in a table:

|  | Singular | Plural |
|---|---|---|
| 1st person | I | We |
| 2nd person | You | You |
| 3rd person | He, she, it | They |

# Exercise 10.4 ✏️

Write the following sentences, choosing a pronoun from the choice in brackets. Decide if the sentence is written in the **first** or **third person**. Write in brackets after each sentence (1) for first person or (3) for third person, depending on the choice you have made.

1. When Michael woke up, ____ felt tired and poorly. *(he / I)*

2. When Maia saw the alligator, ____ thought it was a log floating in the water. *(I / she)*

3. The Indian children waved when ____ saw Maia going past. *(we / they)*

4. I felt tired but ____ wasn't going to give up yet. *(I / he)*

5. ____ could feel the oil and grease under my feet as I walked along the deck. *(he / I)*

Stories can be written as either first or third person narrative. If you are using the first person ('I'), readers have the impression that your main character is talking directly to them. This makes for a friendly, cosy read. However, with the first person, it is difficult to describe what another character in the story is thinking, because you have only one person's point of view.

If you write in the third person ('he, she, they') then the narration may seem less personal, but you are able to switch between different points of view and to share the thoughts of all your characters as if you were hovering above them.

Remember! Whether you choose to write in the **first** or **third** person, you must keep to it. Never make the mistake of saying 'he' and then switching to 'I' for the same character later on in the story.

## Past and present tense

Look at the following sentences, the first of which is taken from *Dawn on Board*:

*It **is** cool, the river **is** dead flat, like glass or mother-of-pearl.*

*It **was** cool, the river **was** dead flat, like glass or mother-of-pearl.*

In the first sentence the writer uses the present tense ('is') to describe the surroundings. It feels as if he is there at the scene and talking to us as the action unfolds.

In the second example the past tense ('was') gives the effect that the writer is remembering his journey after he has returned home. It has already happened.

Many travel accounts (diaries, or journals) are written in the present tense. This makes them feel very alive, like an instant TV or radio programme.

Most stories are written in the past tense (like *Journey to River Sea*). However, some short stories and novels use the present tense.

Remember! Whether you begin with the past or present tense, you must keep to it.

. . . . . . . . . . . . . . . . . . . . . . . . . . . . . . . . . . . . . . . . . . . . . . . . . . .

## Exercise 10.5 

Copy the following sentences, inserting the past or present tense of each verb.

1. In places the river was so wide that she _____ why it was called the River Sea. *(to understand)*

2. The Indian children came out onto the landing stage and _____. *(to wave)*

3. The sun emerges from a belt of cloud and _____ out white-hot. *(to burst)*

**4.** The journey down the Amazon was one that Maia never _____.
*(to forget)*

**5.** It is five a.m. and I _____ tired. *(to feel)*

# Exercise 10.6 🖉

The following paragraph, taken from *Journey to the River Sea,* is written using the third person and the past tense. Rewrite it in the style of Eva Ibbotson's journal using the first person and present tense. You will need to begin with the words 'We pass...'

They passed plantations of rubber trees and Indian villages with the houses built on stilts to stop them being flooded when the river rose. The Indian children came out onto the landing stage and waved and called out, and Maia waved back and didn't stop till they were out of sight.

Sometimes the boat went close enough to the shore for them to pass by old houses owned by the sugar planters or coffee exporters; they could see the verandas with the families taking tea, and dogs stretched out in the shade, and hanging baskets of scarlet flowers.

*(From Journey to the River Sea by Eva Ibbotson)*

# Can you spell?
## Double letters
In the excerpt from *Journey to the River Sea* the writer mentions **crocodiles** and **alligators**.

Lots of people misspell crocodile by putting a double 'c' in the middle. There are many other words like this which feel as if they should have more double letters than they actually do. Look at the following examples:

tomorrow         disappeared         occasion

necessary        process

Did you think *tomorrow* had a double 'm'? Or perhaps you might have put a double 's' in *occasion*. Words like these can be quite tricky.

There are other words which don't seem to need double letters but they actually do have. For example, people often write *alligator* with only one 'l'.

Look at the following words which have double letters, but are often misspelt.

apparatus          alliteration          approximate

success            marriage             immigration

In the words above the second double letter – appearing in blue – is often missed out.

. . . . . . . . . . . . . . . . . . . . . . . . . . . . . . . . . . . . . . . . . . . . . . . .

# Exercise 10.7 ✏

Take another look at the following words used in previous examples. Write a sentence for each of them to show that you understand what they mean as well as how they are spelt. Use a dictionary if you need to. Be careful to copy each word correctly, putting double letters only when they are needed.

1. tomorrow

2. occasion

3. process

4. apparatus

5. approximate

6. immigration

. . . . . . . . . . . . . . . . . . . . . . . . . . . . . . . . . . . . . . . . . . . . . . . .

# Exercise 10.8 ✏

The following words are often misspelt. Can you spell them correctly? First, you will have to solve the clues in brackets to work out what they are.

1. ac----ory   (to go with a dress)

2. op-------ty   (a chance to do something)

3.  ac-------tion    (somewhere to stay)

4.  ex---sive   (too much)

5.  imp----ble  (cannot be done)

# Speaking and listening

1.  Work with a partner.  One of you must imagine you are Maia from *Journey to the River Sea*, or Michael from *River Journeys*. You decide to telephone a friend to share your experience with him or her. Your partner plays the part of the friend at the other end of the telephone line.  He, or she, must ask lots of interesting questions to find out more about the trip.

2.  In groups of about four or five make up a story together about an exciting boat trip down the Amazon.  Sit in a circle and take turns at making up a line of narration, gradually passing the storyline around the group. Remember to use lots of interesting adjectives to describe the river setting and to bring the animals to life along the way.

3.  Imagine you are working for a holiday company. Your task is to prepare a short radio advertisement for a new holiday package in which tourists can enjoy an exciting river safari along the Congo. Your advertisement must be just half a minute long, so keep it short, snappy and very exciting. Think about the sights, sounds and activities on offer, as well as the cost of accommodation and flights.

4.  How good is your memory?  Are you a good listener?  In a large circle of friends, take turns in reciting the following line: *Last summer I went sailing down the Amazon and I saw ...* When it is your turn fill in the blank with the name of an animal, or land feature, you might see along the river, but before you do you must recall and recite all those that have gone before.

# Have you read?

The following stories involve exciting journeys or voyages of discovery. You may have been to some of the places they feature.

*The Amazon (World's Rivers)* by Julia Waterlow, D Rodgers and D Cumming (Hodder Wayland)
*The River* by Rumer Godden (Pan)
*River Boy* by Tim Bowler (Oxford University Press)
*The River at Greene Knowe* by Lucy M. Boston (Faber Children's Books)
*Kensuke's Kingdom* by Michael Morpurgo (Heinemann)
*We Didn't Mean to go to Sea* by Arthur Ransome (Jonathan Cape)
*The Dolphin Crossing* by Jill Paton Walsh (Puffin Books)
*Jungle Islands* by Deborah Pearson (Annick Press)
*'Endurance' Shackleton's Incredible Voyage* by Alfred Lansing (Phoenix)
*Follow the River* by James Alexander Thom (Ballantine)
*Minnow on the Say* by Philippa Pearce
(Oxford University Press)

# Other things to do...

- Write a poem entitled 'My river journey' in which you pretend you are Maia in the passage above and record the sights and sounds of your trip in a poem. You may add other exciting animals too. Remember to include lots of interesting adjectives, adverbs, similes and metaphors to bring the poem to life and to enable your readers to imagine they are on the river with you.

- Find out more about the Amazon. Where is it in the world? What sort of landscape does it pass through? How do people make a living from its resources? Use the Internet, CD ROMs, encyclopaedias and magazines to find out all you can about this most dramatic river.

- Do you remember the work you did on the first and third person narrative? This time, rewrite Michael Wood's account of his journey along the Congo using the **third** person narrative. Remember to change the word 'I' to 'he' or 'Michael'. Once you have rewritten the passage, think about how it has changed. Is it more or less immediate? What effect does this version have on the impression of Michael Wood's character?

# Galore Park

## JUNIOR SERIES

**GALORE PARK**

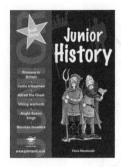

- Perfect for working towards Key Stage 2 and Common Entrance at 11+

- Suitable for the specialist or non specialist teacher or parent

- Rigorous, challenging material to stretch pupils

- Clear explanations and worked examples

- Plenty of exercises to ensure pupils have understood each topic

- Answer books also available

- Full of practical activities and interesting facts

For more information please visit our website:

# www.galorepark.co.uk

    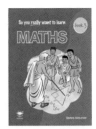